THE BEDBUG AND SELECTED POETRY

КЛОП
СТИХИ
ПОЭМЫ

translated by Max Hayward and George Reavey

VLADIMIR MAYAKOVSKY

THE BEDBUG AND SELECTED POETRY

edited with an introduction by Patricia Blake

INDIANA UNIVERSITY PRESS

BLOOMINGTON

First Midland Book Edition 1975

Published in Canada by Fitzhenry & Whiteside Limited, Don Mills,
Ontario. Manufactured in the United States of America.

Library of Congress Cataloging in Publication Data

Maiakovskiĭ, Vladimir Vladimirovich, 1894-1930.
    The bedbug [a play] and selected poetry.

    Poems in English and Russian.
    Reprint of the 1960 ed. published by Meridian Books, New York.
    Includes bibliographical references.
    I. Title.
PG3476.M3A24 1975   891.7'1'42   75-10805
ISBN 0-253-31130-6
ISBN 0-253-20189-6 pbk.   7 8 9 10 94 93 92 91

Note on Translations and Text

George Reavey translated all the Russian poetry in this book, except *Conversation with a Tax Collector about Poetry,* which was translated by Max Hayward, who also translated *The Bedbug.* The notes to the poetry and the play are by the editor, Patricia Blake.

The Russian text of the poems is from Vladimir Mayakovsky, *Complete Works,* Izd. Khudozhestvennoi Literatury, Moscow, 1955-8, except *Past One O'clock* . . . , which is from *Complete Works,* Goslitizdat, Moscow, 1939-47.

Acknowledgments

I would like to express my warm thanks to Mrs. Tatiana Yakovleva, and also to the many friends and former colleagues of Mayakovsky's, in the Soviet Union and elsewhere, who very generously provided me with biographical material. I am indebted to Max Hayward for his great practical assistance, and, above all, for his compelling enthusiasm and interest in this book. Mr. Hayward wishes to express his gratitude to the Russian Research Center at Harvard University, where he completed his translation of *The Bedbug.*

PATRICIA BLAKE

CONTENTS

Introduction
The Two Deaths of Vladimir Mayakovsky
by Patricia Blake

Early in the morning of April 14, 1930, the Russian poet Semyon Kirsanov telephoned Vladimir Mayakovsky and asked him for the name of his tailor in Moscow. Mayakovsky, who was something of a dandy, invited Kirsanov to join him at the tailor's the following day.

Now, that morning had begun like many others in Mayakovsky's life. He had made a date with one of his literary friends; some lines of a poem he had been playing with for months had at last come clear in his mind; and he was again contemplating the act that had obsessed him all his life. In observance of the Russian superstition that before death a man must put on clean linen, he changed his shirt. On his desk he placed a letter he had prepared two days before. But still he was undecided. He placed a single cartridge in the cylinder of his revolver; twice before he had played Russian roulette with himself and won. That day, at 10:15 a.m., he lost his life in the game. The final version of the verses he left behind reads: "And, as they say, the incident is closed./Love's boat has smashed against the daily grind./Now life and I are quits. Why bother then/to balance mutual sorrows, pains, and hurts."

His friend Boris Pasternak has described the hours that followed:

Between eleven and twelve the ripples were still circling around the shot. The news rocked the telephones, blanketed faces with pallor, and directed one to the Lubyansky Passage, through the yard and into the house, where already people from the town and the tenants packed all the way up the staircase wept and pressed against each other, pitched there and splashed on the walls by the flattening force of events. . . . On the threshold Aseyev was crying. . . . In the depths of the room by the window, his head drawn into his shoulders, Kirsanov stood, shaken by noiseless sobs. . . . A lump rose in my throat. I decided to cross over to his room again, this time to cry my fill. . . . He lay on his side with his face to the wall, sullen and imposing, with a sheet up to his chin, his mouth half open as in sleep. Haughtily turning his back on all, even in this repose, even in this sleep, he was stubbornly straining to go away somewhere. His face took one back to the days when he had called himself "handsome, twentytwoyearold," for here death has arrested an attitude which it almost never succeeds in capturing. This was an expression with which one begins life but does not end it. He was sulking and indignant.●

For Pasternak and the other young writers of Russia's splendidly creative twenties, Mayakovsky's death, at the age of thirty-six, was cause for desolation and foreboding. His suicide was one of those rare acts of definition in history which strips clean a whole era and mercilessly lays open the future. The poet who had tried to place his supremely individual gifts at the service of a collective society now lay with a bullet through his heart—"love's boat . . . smashed against the daily grind." While he lived his voice had roused the talent of an entire generation of Russian poets. After his death, his colleagues were soon silenced or forced to yield their originality to the demands of socialist realism—when they were not obliterated altogether by the purges of the thirties.

Nowadays the sense of Mayakovsky's suicide has been muddled by crude interpretation. Communist

● *Safe Conduct* (1931). Passage translated by George Reavey.

critics dismiss it as an outrageous, an improper, or, at best, an inexplicable accident. Abroad, the view is favored that he was driven to death by Party hacks who are said to have persecuted him in the late twenties. Romantics suggest that he killed himself over a woman, while realists maintain that he succumbed to a grave mental illness.

The truth, however, lies not so much in the conditions of his death as in the circumstances of his life. Mayakovsky, the poet laureate of the Soviet state, was, in effect, the most alienated figure in Russian literature. Not even Gogol, not even Dostoevsky had known the singular desolation of Mayakovsky. At twenty-two, he had already found its definition: "But where can a man/like me/bury his head?/Where is there shelter for me?/. . . The gold of all the Californias/will never satisfy the rapacious horde of my lusts./. . . I shall go by,/dragging my burden of love./In what delirious/and ailing night,/was I sired by Goliaths—/ I, so large,/so unwanted?" •

Much of Mayakovsky's life was squandered in the search for some refuge from the pain that hounded him. He sought it in the absolutes of his time—the Bolshevik revolution and the theology of communism —and these ultimately failing him, in death. During his life he was engaged in a performance which he described in these terms: "I shall plunge head first from the scaffolding of days./Over the abyss I've stretched my soul in a tightrope/and, juggling with words, totter above it." •• Mass audiences were required for all the parts he assumed in this performance: revolutionist, propagandist, cartoonist, journalist, actor, screen-

• *To His Beloved Self, the Author Dedicates These Lines* (1916).
•• *The Backbone Flute* (1915).

writer, and, often enough, poet. For nearly fifteen years the most excruciatingly personal of poets traveled from city to city across Russia giving lectures and declaiming his verses.

Inevitably his work reflects this prodigality. He produced some of the most splendid lyrics in Russian poetry and, in the same breath, some of the silliest doggerel in Soviet propaganda history. He wasted his talent drawing posters, and composing thousands of slogans and "agitational" jingles that urged the Soviet people to drink boiled water, put their money in the bank, and patronize state stores. According to Mayakovsky, his slogan, "Nowhere but in Mosselprom," a Soviet equivalent to "Nobody but nobody undersells Gimbels," was poetry of the highest order. The author of *The Bedbug* and *The Bathhouse,* two brilliant dramatic satires on the philistinism and bureaucratic idiocies of Soviet society, was also capable of writing, without irony: "I want/a commissar/with a decree/ to lean over the thought of the age./. . . I want/the factory committee/to lock/my lips/when the work is done." •

As Mayakovsky was all things to himself, so he was to his readers. Lenin had no use for him. Stalin declared he was the most talented poet of the Soviet epoch. Pasternak, who can hardly be said to share Stalin's taste, called him the foremost poet of his generation. Another distinguished Nobel Prize winner, Ivan Bunin, dismissed him as a versifying hooligan. These contradictions have endured. Today, Mayakovsky's chauvinistic *My Soviet Passport* and elegiac *Vladimir Ilyich Lenin* are taught in all Soviet schools. At the same time he is the idol of the young poets and writers who are straining against the orthodoxy of

• *Back Home!* (1925).

socialist realism; thirty years after his death, such poems as *I* and *The Cloud in Trousers* are considered by them as models of unorthodoxy.

Everybody is right about Mayakovsky. In the thirteen volumes of his complete works, about one third consists of fulminations on patriotic and political themes. Another third is composed of serious "revolutionary" poems which are quite original in their genre and which still today can evoke some of the fervor of the early years of the Bolshevik revolution. What remains are his satiric plays and his lyrics on the themes that were central to Mayakovsky's life: a man's longing for love and his suffering at the hands of the loveless; his passion for life and his desolation in a hostile and inhuman world; his yearning for the absolutes of human experience and his rage at his impotent self.

The works that appear in this volume have not been selected to represent the entire range of Mayakovsky's preoccupations, but for their relevance to literature. These include his best realized play, *The Bedbug,* and a selection from his lyrics, which alternated with his political utterances from 1913, the year of his first published book of verse, until his death in 1930. Also included are a few of his nonlyrical poems, such as *Back Home!* and *At the Top of My Voice,* which are particularly characteristic or which have a bearing on his personal tragedy.

Only odds and ends are known about the early life of this wild man of Russian letters. (A friend of his once remarked that Mayakovsky's memory was like the road to Poltava—everyone left his galoshes along it.) His laconic autobiography, *I Myself,* and some of his poems suggest, however, that Mayakovsky's great themes—the loneliness and lovelessness of man—were established long before manhood. In "As a Boy," the second poem in the cycle *I Love,* Mayakovsky recalled: "I was gifted in measure with love./Since childhood,/people/have been drilled to labor./But I/fled to the banks of the Rion/and knocked about there,/doing absolutely nothing./Mamma chided me angrily:/'Good for nothing!'/Papa threatened to belt me." A motif of Mayakovsky's verse is an anguished appeal to his mother: "Mamma!/Your son is gloriously ill!/Mamma!/His heart is on fire./ Tell his sisters, Lyuda and Olya,/he has no place to hide in." • The father frequently offers a terrifying image: " 'Sun!/Father mine!/If at least *thou* wouldst have mercy and stop tormenting me!/For my blood thou spilled gushes down this nether road.' " ••

Mayakovsky evidently found little to sustain him in the world of his childhood. By his own account he was a lonely, restless, and troublemaking child. He felt confined by Bagdadi (now renamed Mayakovsky), the Georgian village where he was born in 1893. The splendors of the Caucasus which had so moved Pushkin and Lermontov only bored Mayakovsky. When he was seven, his father, an impoverished Russian nobleman reduced to the job of forest ranger, began to take the boy with him on his rounds. During one such excursion, Mayakovsky glimpsed a rivet factory stunningly illuminated in the night. "After seeing electricity," he wrote in his autobiography, "I lost interest in nature. Not up to date enough."

School bored him equally. He very nearly failed his high school entrance exam by confusing an ancient Church Slavonic word with a Georgian word. "So

• *The Cloud in Trousers* (1915).
•• *I* (1913).

14

I conceived a hatred for everything ancient, everything churchy, and everything Slavonic," he noted later, with characteristic exaggeration. "Possibly from this spring my futurism, my atheism, and my internationalism." •

It was in 1905 that he first discovered a remedy for boredom: revolution. At the age of twelve he was stealing his father's sawed-off shotguns and delivering them to the local Social Democratic committee. At fifteen, when he had moved to Moscow, he joined the Bolshevik faction and carried out underground propaganda among bakers, shoemakers, and printers until his arrest in 1908. As it turned out, the eleven months he served in prison were immensely valuable; he spent them reading, or, as he put it, "disposing of" contemporary authors and "plunging" into Shakespeare, Byron, and Tolstoy. Greatly agitated by his reading, he was determined to drop politics in favor of the arts. "The authors I had read were the so-called great ones," he reflected in his autobiography, "but how easy to write better than they! I had already acquired a correct attitude toward the world. I needed only experience in art. Where would I find it? I was half-baked. . . . It was all right for others to be in the Party. They had a university behind them. . . . What could I set up against the aesthetics of the past that had avalanched on me?"

Disgusted by his first attempts at poetry, he dabbled in abstract painting for a while until David Burlyuk, the futurist painter, talked him into his destiny. Mayakovsky met Burlyuk one night on a Moscow boulevard and showed him a poem, which he tried to pass off as having been written by a friend.

• *I Myself*, in *Mayakovsky and His Poetry*, Pilot Press, London, 1942.

15

Burlyuk shouted: "You wrote it yourself. You're a genius!" "This grandiose and undeserved appellation overjoyed me," wrote Mayakovsky. "I became immersed in poetry. That evening quite suddenly I became a poet."

Henceforth Burlyuk introduced him all over town as "my friend, the genius, the famous poet, Mayakovsky." As it happened, Mayakovsky arrived on the Moscow artistic scene at the precise moment in history when Moscow was readiest for Mayakovsky. The coincidence of his talent and temperament with the dynamics of the period was absolute; no other writer so perfectly embodied the fearful tensions of the last decade of the empire.

When Mayakovsky burst on stage in 1911, he found himself in a Moscow seized with the frenzy of modernism. Many writers, painters, musicians, and theater directors had caught up with the Western avant-garde movements, and already such people as Malevich, Kandinsky, Chagall, Prokofiev, and Meyerhold threatened to surpass their European colleagues with the brilliance and originality of their experiments. Talented young people, who had thronged to the capital from the provinces, had formed dozens of competing modernist groups and circles and met nightly to debate their manifestoes for a revolution in the arts.

Revolution, as seen by these intellectuals and artists, had little in common with the vision held by Lenin, then waiting expectantly in exile. Their rebellion was directed largely against the suffocating conservatism and authoritarianism of imperial Russia. For many, the target was merely symbolism, the dominant aesthetic movement since 1900, which had promised Russia a great poetic revival. But the symbolist writers and poets had of late grown too stuffy, too esoteric for the younger generation. The acmeist literary circle, for example, countered the symbolists' woolly mysticism with the slogan, "Art is solidity, firmness."

In reality, these feverish young intellectuals were stricken, as all Russia was stricken, by a sense of the impending cataclysm. Alexander Blok has described the mood: "I think that there lay upon the hearts of the people of the last few generations a constant and wanton feeling of catastrophe, which was evoked by an impressive accumulation of indisputable facts, some of which have already passed into history and others still awaiting accomplishment. . . . In us all is a feeling of sickness, of alarm, of catastrophe, of disruption." •

No wonder then that Mayakovsky soon became a commanding figure among the Russian intelligentsia only a few years after Burlyuk's introduction. Who else but Mayakovsky could so convincingly exploit a feeling of sickness, alarm, catastrophe, and disruption? Characteristically, his choice among the modernist movements active in Russia was futurism—the most aggressive and extravagant of them all. Like their Italian counterparts, the Russian futurists wanted to shatter every artistic convention and set up forms that would be appropriate to the machine age. Their manifesto of 1912, signed by Mayakovsky, reads in part:

We alone are the *Face of Our Time*. Time's trumpet blares in our art of words. The past is stifling. The Academy and Pushkin are more unintelligible than hieroglyphs. Throw Pushkin, Dostoevsky, Tolstoy, etc., overboard from

• "Nature and Culture" (1908), in *The Spirit of Music*, Lindsay Drummond Ltd., London, 1946.

the steamer of modernity. . . . All these Maxim Gorkys, Bloks, Sologubs, Remizovs, Averchenkos, Chernys, Kuzmins, etc., etc.—all they want is a villa by the river. . . . From the height of skyscrapers we look down on their insignificance. We demand respect for the poet's right (1) to enlarge the vocabulary with arbitrary and derivative words—neologisms; (2) to uncompromising hatred for the language used hitherto; (3) to tear with horror from their proud heads the crowns of worthless fame made of bathroom brushes; (4) to stand upon the rock of the word *"We"* in a sea of cat-calls and indignation. •

Indeed, the futurists liked nothing better than cat-calls and indignation. Their favorite entertainment was shocking the bourgeois. They amused themselves by crashing and breaking up respectable private concerts, exhibitions, and poetry readings, their faces painted with landscapes and wearing bizarre costumes. Their work was equally anarchic. The painters declared that the object of art was not to transform or to reflect nature but to deform it. The writers announced that words had to be freed from meaning and a new "trans-sense" language created to replace everyday speech. Velimir Khlebnikov, for example, composed ingeniously unintelligible verses, such as his famous laughter poem, which was made up entirely of variations on the root *smekh*—laughter.

Unlike his colleagues, Mayakovsky was a futurist for the fun of it. "Trans-sense" experiments did not appeal to him; what he loved was futurism's anarchic spirit. On the eve of revolution, Mayakovsky could often be found in some public hall or theater, wearing a top hat, a large wooden spoon in his lapel as a boutonnière, and carrying a gold-topped cane, reciting his

• Translated by C. M. Bowra in *The Creative Experiment*, Grove Press, New York, 1948.

verses through a megaphone: "No gray hairs streak my soul,/no grandfatherly fondness there!/I shake the world with the might of my voice,/and walk—handsome,/twentytwoyearold." •

Moscow, at least, was shaken by Mayakovsky. He was a formidable spectacle. Over six feet tall and built like a boxer, he lowered over everyone like a storm cloud. A scruffy shock of dark hair tumbled over his deeply lined forehead. His thick lower lip curved toward the left, insolently, in conversation. In manner, he appeared alternately morose and exuberant, taciturn and witty, cruel and supremely gentle. But whatever his posture, his genius was unmistakeable—a goad to some and an insult to others. The young iconoclasts of Moscow were spellbound by him, respectable people were scandalized, while women of every sort found him irresistible.

Pasternak has described his stunning first impressions of Mayakovsky in 1914:

He sat on a chair as on the saddle of a motorcycle, leant forward, sliced and rapidly swallowed a Wiener Schnitzel, played cards, shifted his eyes without turning his head, strolled solemnly along the Kuznetsky, hummed sonorously and nasally, as though they were fragments of liturgy, some very deep-pondered scraps of his own and other people's work, frowned, grew, drove about and read in public; and, in the background of all this, as though in the wake of some skater dashing straight forward, there always loomed some particular day of his own, which had preceded all the days gone by—the day on which he had made his astonishing flying start that gave him the look of being so hugely unbent and unconstrained. His way of carrying himself suggested something like a decision when it has been executed and its consequences are irrevocable. This decision was his very genius; his encounter with it had so astonished

• *The Cloud in Trousers* (1915).

him at some time that it had since become his prescribed theme for all time, and he had devoted his whole being to incarnate it without any pity or reserve.●

Ivan Bunin had quite another impression. In his memoirs, the novelist tells of meeting Mayakovsky at the formal opening of an exhibition of Finnish painters in Petrograd, between the February and October revolutions:

The "flower of the Russian intelligentsia" was there to a man: famous painters, actors, writers, ministers, deputies, and one high foreign diplomat, namely the French ambassador. . . . I sat at supper with Gorky and the Finnish painter Axel Gallen, and Mayakovsky began his performance by suddenly coming up to us, pushing a chair between ours and helping himself from our plates and drinking out of our glasses. Gallen stared at him spellbound, just as he would probably have stared if a horse had been led into the banquet hall . . . at that moment Milyukov, our Foreign Minister at the time, rose for an official toast and Mayakovsky dashed towards him, to the center of the table, jumped on a chair and shouted something so obscene that Milyukov was completely flabbergasted. After a moment, regaining his control, he tried to start his speech again, "Ladies and gentlemen . . ." but Mayakovsky yelled louder than ever, and Milyukov shrugged his shoulders and sat down. Then the French ambassador rose to his feet. He was obviously convinced that the Russian hooligan would give in to him. What a hope! His voice was drowned by a deafening bellow from Mayakovsky. But this was not all. A wild and senseless pandemonium broke out. Mayakovsky supporters also began to yell, pounding their feet on the floor and their fists on the tables. They screamed with laughter, whined, squeaked, snorted. But suddenly all this was quashed by a truly tragic wail of one of the Finns, a painter, who looked like a clean-shaven sea-lion. Rather

● *Safe Conduct* (1931). Passage translated by George Reavey.

drunk, pale as death, he had obviously been shaken to the core by this excess of misbehavior, and started to shout at the top of his voice, literally with tears in his eyes, one of the few Russian words he knew:

"*Mnogo! Mno-go! Mno-go!*" ("many" or "much"). •

Mnogo. Mayakovsky was clearly too much for a lot of people, and not merely because of his manners. His futurist antics aside, Mayakovsky represented an affront to the values and sensibilities of the liberal intelligentsia. For all those who cared for the sweet and solemn diction of Russian verse, Mayakovsky sounded a monstrous clangor. His thumping rhythms, his declamatory style, his use of puns, neologisms, and *outré* images shattered every standard of verbal behavior. But more importantly, for all those who cherished the Russian intelligentsia's humanistic traditions, there was something horrifying about Mayakovsky's self-absorption—his craving for melodrama, his penchant for high tragedy, and his fascination with the drumbeat of revolution.

In effect, he appeared as a traitor to the old intelligentsia, and, even worse, as the symbol of the ultimate failure of its mission. Since Pushkin, the writer, and especially the poet, had acted as the conscience of autocratic Russia and as the spokesman for the aspirations of the great mass of illiterate Russian people. It was the liberal intelligentsia that had first given the people a national consciousness, brought the ideas of Europe's Enlightenment to backward Russia, and, like Pushkin, "celebrated freedom in this cruel age." But, as revolution neared, the intelligentsia was losing contact with the people, now roused to the brink of violence. "We see ourselves . . . flying in a light rickety aeroplane, high above the earth," wrote Blok

• *Memories and Portraits,* John Lehmann, London, 1951.

21

in 1908. "But beneath us is a rumbling and fire-spitting mountain and down its sides behind clouds of ashes, roll streams of red-hot lava." • It was left to Mayakovsky to be the poet of this eruption.

Although ultimately correct, this judgment of Mayakovsky was premature before October 1917. True, his harsh and violent idiom was far closer to the mood of elemental Russia than the elegant language of the "gentlemen poets" who warbled (in Mayakovsky's phrase) of "pages, palaces, love and lilac blooms." ••
Yet in his early poetry he was almost entirely absorbed by his personal torments. Then, it was Pasternak, of all the writers bound to the humanistic tradition, who understood Mayakovsky best. Later, Pasternak was to reject his political verse, but in Mayakovsky's early lyrics he saw "poetry molded by a master; proud and daemonic and at the same time infinitely doomed, at the point of death, almost an appeal for help." •••

Indeed, from these lyrics rises a single cry of pain, at times barely tolerable to the human ear. His poetic techniques served above all to sharpen the impact of his feelings on the senses of the reader—or rather, of the listener, for his verses were written to be read aloud. However complex the structure of language and meter, the effect is always immediate; Mayakovsky had an extraordinary ear for the language of the street, and the art to transform it into a perfectly original yet familiar idiom. This is why he reached a much larger audience than most modernist poets.

With such elements as street slang, popular songs, and *chastushki* (satirical jingles of the industrial age)

• "Nature and Culture," in *The Spirit of Music*, Lindsay Drummond Ltd., London, 1946.
•• *Brother Writers* (1917).
••• *An Essay in Autobiography*, Collins and Harvill Press, London, 1959.

Mayakovsky created a personal style involving grammatical deformations, bizarre inversions, neologisms, and puns. He was most ingenious in coining new verbal forms with, as he called it, "the small change of suffixes and flections." The result is not so esoteric as it would be in English; spoken Russian yields far more gracefully than English to the inventor. Few of Mayakovsky's verbal innovations can therefore be rendered in English.

Equally unrenderable are Mayakovsky's rhymes. In *Conversation with a Tax Collector about Poetry*, he calls his rhyme "a keg of dynamite" and his line "a fuse" which "burns to the end/and explodes,/and the town/is blown sky-high/in a strophe." In his essay "How to Make Verse" (1926), he explains: "I always put the most characteristic word at the end of a line and find for it a rhyme at any cost. As a result my rhymes are almost always out of the ordinary and, in any case, have not been used before me and do not exist in rhyming dictionaries." Assonances, off-rhymes, punning rhymes, or mere echoes served Mayakovsky's purpose. The Russian critic Dmitri Mirsky suggested that an English equivalent of a conservative Mayakovskian rhyme would be Browning's "ranunculus" with "Tommy-make-room-for-your-uncle-us."

His stunning imagery, however, breaks through in translation. Bold, extreme, and frequently brutal, his images constitute his most effective means of communication. He was a master of metaphor and hyperbole. In fact many of his poems, such as *The Cloud in Trousers,* are entirely composed of metaphors. Some of these metaphors recur constantly in the lyrical portion of his work: Mayakovsky is impaled on spires, trampled by madmen or mobs, consumed by fire, or swept away by storms. In his more buoyant moods, he is fond of measuring himself with the elements: the ocean's wave, thunder, and sun. In *An Extraordinary Adventure* he invites the sun to tea, and slapping him on the back, proclaims: "To shine—/and to hell with everything else!/That is my motto—/and the sun's!"

Few of his lyrics are so sunny. At the age of twenty, in his poem *I*, he was already "thrusting the dagger of desperate words/into the swollen pulp of the sky." This splendid poem, like many of Mayakovsky's earliest verses, shows the influence of the futurists' experiments. Not wholly intelligible for this reason, it nonetheless suggests in its imagery ("midnight/with sodden hands has fingered/me") the mood of the author. Later, Mayakovsky was more explicit; in his most important work before 1917, *The Cloud in Trousers,* he is directly concerned with the agony of love. He begins with an attack on the sentimental drawing-room poets who cannot turn themselves inside out. Then he proceeds to do just that. Rejected by "Maria" in Part 1, he eviscerates first himself and ultimately the universe. His screams claw his mouth apart, a nerve leaps within him like a sick man from his bed. He will root up his soul and, trampling it to a bloody rag, offer it to Maria as a banner. "Look!" he cries, "again they've beheaded the stars,/and the sky is bloodied with carnage!" Here, in these images of terror and violence, is Mayakovsky at his best and worst. Most often he is the master of his material, but sometimes he loses control and staggers out of the bounds of art into the realm of psychopathology. Then the poet's anguish appears unnecessary, excessive, artificial. It is at such moments that Mayakovsky's great weakness is most apparent. This weakness lay not in the overabundance of passion but, all too often, in the absence of it. "I am bored, deadly bored," he always complained to his friends. Clearly, he felt a deadness in himself which demanded quickening. Hence, he was constantly exacerbating his feelings; only when he had thus roused himself to an extremity of emotion did he feel wholly alive. All the extravagances of this astonishing man's life—his dramatic involvements with women, his intoxication with Bolshevism, and paradoxically, even his obsession with suicide—must be understood in this sense.

Inevitably, Mayakovsky's work suffered from the same extravagance. Poetry was his confessional, his lectern, and his soapbox. Here he always assumed the first person, the "I" with which he could directly assail his audience with every detail of his personal affairs, and every nuance of his feelings. His verse, in short, resembled him absolutely.

Mayakovsky's misfortunes in love, which constitute the main topic of his lyrical poetry, were either invented or invited. The two unloving "Marias" of Odessa and Moscow were, for example, far more yielding to him in life than in *The Cloud in Trousers*. In fact most women adored him; he was handsome, he was famous, and he had the ineluctable charm of a *poète maudit* in the rough. And, according to Mayakovsky, he adored them equally. As an adolescent, he loved to boast of his successes. He once told Burlyuk: "The greatest pleasure is to wait in clean bedclothes for the arrival of the female species." Yet, in reality, he quickly abandoned women who loved him simply or easily. In love, as in all things, Mayakovsky favored the impossible. He always chose women who were unavailable to him for some reason or other. He had two important loves in his life, both unrealized, both doomed from the start.

The first of these loves was Lily Brik—the famous

Lily whose coldness and inconstancy Mayakovsky lamented in public for fifteen years. Lily, the handsome and cultivated daughter of a Moscow lawyer, was the wife of Osip Brik, the critic and editor. In their home they maintained a permanent literary salon where for many years Lily collected famous men from the avant-garde, much as she added to her wardrobe of splendid dresses from the Paris couturiers. Mayakovsky first met this captivating creature in July 1915—"a most joyful date," he noted in his autobiography. A few months later he dedicated to Lily what is surely the most savage indictment of a woman and womanhood to be formulated in our time: *The Backbone Flute*. From Lily's bed rises the smell of scorching wool —the devil's flesh rising in sulphurous flames. Lily's lips are a monastery hacked from frigid rock. Lily's eyes excavate the hollows of two graves in her face. And why? Lily, the terrible, the accursed Lily has left Mayakovsky for another man. He is condemned to the Siberia of the heart where, he writes, "I'll scratch Lily's name on my fetters,/and in the darkness of hard labor, kiss them again and again."

The Backbone Flute is merely a premonition. Lily and he were not even lovers in 1915. Not until after the Revolution did Lily, her complaisant husband, and Mayakovsky begin living as a *ménage à trois,* and not until 1923 did Lily abandon him for another man. Yet he was always a step ahead of tragedy; his lyrics were composed in apprehension of it. In *The Backbone Flute* he suggests that it would be better for him to punctuate his end with a bullet. In *Man* (1916-17) he writes: "The heart yearns for a bullet/while the throat raves of a razor/. . . . The soul shivers;/she's caught in ice,/and there's no escape for her!" His "handcuffs rattle" as he foresees the millennium of love when all will perish, God will burn out the last rays of the sun, and only Mayakovsky's pain will survive and be intensified. He concludes: "And I stand/wrapped in flames/at the imperishable stake/of my inconceivable love."

The stake, fetters, handcuffs—these images suggest the nature of Mayakovsky's bond with Lily Brik. It consisted largely of mutually imposed indignities. The poems he wrote in her name and recited, with her permission, all over the country, were nearly always abusive. After her infidelity and the end of their love affair, he continued to share an apartment with the Briks—a stormy arrangement that lasted until his death. During his travels and hers, he bombarded her with letters and telegrams, addressed to "Kitten" and signed "Puppy," which begged for some scrap of affection.• The fact that he continued to send these communications long after he was involved with other women, suggests that he had invented her to serve his masochism. She herself was aware of her insubstantial role. To his last plaintive messages wired to her a month before his death, she replied: "I have received your little telegram . . . but I do not understand to whom you are writing—certainly not to me. . . . Please invent a new text for telegrams."

Tough, vain, and basically insensible, Lily was well insulated against Mayakovsky, but frailer souls often suffered because of him. People with suicidal inclinations were particularly vulnerable. "Maria" of *The Cloud in Trousers*, Part 3, was in reality, a seventeen-year-old girl, hopelessly in love with Mayakovsky. After a brief affair, he ignored her. A few years later

• These letters, unaccountably released for publication by Lily Brik in 1958, appear in *Literaturnoe nasledstvo*, Vol. 65, *"Novoe o Mayakovskom,"* Moscow, 1958.

she committed suicide. Although Mayakovsky cannot be held responsible for her death, he was guilty of writing a scenario, *How Do You Do?*, in 1926, containing a sequence which satirized it. In the first scene of the movie, the hero, who is named Mayakovsky and acted by Mayakovsky, is comfortably seated in an armchair, sipping tea and reading an account of an attempted suicide in a newspaper. The figure of a girl holding a revolver emerges from the page. With a despairing look she fires a bullet into her temple, "breaking the newspaper as dogs break through paper hoops at the circus. Mayakovsky tries to stop her but it's too late," reads the scenario, "he clutches the paper with an expression of disgust and throws himself back in his chair . . . his face gradually becomes calm."

Mayakovsky's most famous act of cruelty concerned Sergei Esenin. Always a critic of the great and dissolute neo-romantic poet, Mayakovsky was enraged when Esenin committed suicide in 1925. Ravaged by heavy drinking and drugs and disillusioned by the Sovietization of Russia, Esenin had cut his wrists, written a farewell poem in his own blood, then hanged himself. Two lines of this poem read: "in this life to die is nothing new/and, in truth, to live is not much newer."

Mayakovsky promptly composed a poem entitled *To Sergei Esenin* in which he countered: "in this life it is not hard to die,/to mold life is more difficult."

Mayakovsky compounded the injury to Esenin's memory when, a year later, he lectured on his purpose in writing *To Sergei Esenin:* "My aim: to deliberately paralyze the action of Esenin's last lines; to make Esenin's end uninteresting; to set forth, in place of the easy beauty of death, another kind of beauty. For the working class needs strength in order to continue the revolution which demands . . . that we glorify life and the joy that is to be found along that most difficult of roads—the road towards communism." •

Not until Mayakovsky's own suicide four years later could this outrageous utterance be wholly understood. He had, of course, been speaking of his own dilemma. In these crude terms he had defined the alternative that was always present in his mind: the easy beauty of death or the difficult road to communism. The October revolution had promised him a way out of the miasma of his personal life; the *poète maudit* who had indulged in all that was morbid in his temperament might now aspire to a higher order of things: the splendid-sounding ideals of communism. Besides, as his adolescent experiences had proved, revolution was a tonic for the boredom that plagued him.

No wonder then that October 1917 found Mayakovsky issuing "orders" to the "army of art": "Comrades, to the barricades! . . . Streets are our brushes,/squares our palettes!" •• During the first years of the revolution, while hundreds of distinguished intellectuals were fleeing abroad from the terror, and all Russia was suffering the agony of civil war, famine, and epidemics, Mayakovsky was exultant. Of course, many other Russian writers like Blok, Bely, Esenin, and Bryusov were also enthusiasts of the revolution, but most of these were very quickly disabused of the Bolsheviks and vice versa.

At this juncture, it seemed that the liberal intelligentsia had been right about Mayakovsky. Bunin spoke for many of those who were now in geographical or spiritual exile from Soviet Russia when he wrote that Mayakovsky was revelling in luxury and fame

• *How to Make Verse* (1926).
•• *Order to the Army of Art* (1918).

while the Russian people fed on corpses, and that he had abandoned the scandalous behavior of a futurist for the scandalous behavior of a "revolutionary demagogue, a fiery bard of communism and red terror who exhorted Russian youth to 'build their lives on the Dzerzhinsky pattern.'" • Mayakovsky was not revelling in luxury, but it was certainly true that he was unmoved by the inhumanity of the early years of the revolution. The savagery of the terror that had driven even Maxim Gorky to a physical breakdown compounded of grief and horror, left Mayakovsky enraptured, like a man who has had a vision of the second coming of Christ. The metaphor is his own. In *The Cloud in Trousers* he had prophesied the revolution in these terms, underestimating the date by only a year: "I perceive whom no one sees,/crossing the mountains of time./Where men's eyes stop short,/there, at the head of hungry hordes,/the year 1916 cometh/in the thorny crown of revolutions."

As it turned out, however, Mayakovsky fell far short of becoming a New Soviet Man. The dictatorship he had greeted so devoutly soon began to grate on his sensibilities. He felt increasingly oppressed by the Soviet bureaucracy and exasperated by its smugness and philistinism. After the terror and the Civil War, Mayakovsky's attitude toward the authorities alternated between submission and independence. On the one hand, he styled himself as a "loudmouthed rabble-rouser" who served the state with masses of propaganda posters, jingles, and long-winded exhortations in verse, and on the other, he was determined to be the *enfant terrible* of Soviet literature whose mission was to save the state from surrendering to the pharisees and the philistines.

• *Memories and Portraits*, John Lehmann, London, 1951.

Until 1928 at least, he was free to behave pretty much as he willed. From the end of the Civil War until Stalin began dictating cultural life, the artist had considerable independence, and although some of the cream of the intelligentsia had been lost to Russia in emigration, many outstanding people had remained to pursue the artistic experiments begun before the revolution. The great experimental theater of Vsevolod Meyerhold flourished in the twenties, while Bely, Zoshchenko, Zamyatin, Babel, and Pasternak were doing some of their best work. Writers traveled back and forth to London, Paris, Berlin, and Prague, publishing books there and bringing back quantities of Western literature for translation into Russian.

In this liberal atmosphere, Mayakovsky usually managed to retain his originality, even in his crudest polemics and his broadest satires. In *150,000,000,* a poem written during the American intervention in the Russian Civil War, the colossal peasant Ivan, who has 150,000,000 heads, an arm as long as the Neva River, and heels as big as the Caspian steppes, wades across the Atlantic to fight a hand-to-hand battle with a Woodrow Wilson, resplendent in a top hat as high as the Eiffel Tower. In *Paris* (1923), he invites the Eiffel Tower to lead a revolution, then follow him to Moscow where, Mayakovsky tells her tenderly, she will be better scrubbed, polished, and cherished than in her decadent hometown. In *About Conferences* (1922), he observes that at daybreak every office worker disappears into conferences of the "A-B-C-D-E-F-G committees re the purchase of a bottle of ink by the provincial co-op." Annoyed at not finding anyone at his desk by nightfall, Mayakovsky bursts into one such conference and finds that only torsos are in attendance. Lower parts are conferring elsewhere. A clerk informs him that workers have had to split themselves up to meet organizational needs. Mayakovsky's final plea: "Oh, for just one more conference re the eradication of all conferences!"

His impudence to Soviet authorities was famous in Moscow. Roman Grynberg, a friend of Mayakovsky's in the early twenties, gives an arresting example. In 1922, immediately after a meeting with Trotsky, then People's Commissar for War, the poet rushed to his friend to brag about the "historic pun" he had just made at Trotsky's expense. Trotsky had summoned him to his office to interview him on the subject of modern Russian poetry for the book he was then writing, *Literature and Revolution*. Mayakovsky described the work of his colleagues, then Trotsky repeated his account after him, in his own words. "What do you think? How was that as a first try?" asked Trotsky. Mayakovsky answered with a devastating pun: "The first pancake falls like a People's Commissar" (*pervy blin lyog narkomom*), a play on the saying "the first pancake falls like a lump," (*pervy blin lyog komom*).

Although propaganda and satire had become Mayakovsky's main preoccupations after the revolution, he did not by any means abandon lyrical poetry. Only now he was ashamed of his lyrics. "Unfortunately I have again a craving to write lyric verse," he wrote Lily Brik in 1924, shortly after having completed a three thousand line elegy on the death of Lenin. Clearly, he was trying to contain the personal agonies that constantly threatened to spill out into his poetry. His friend Roman Jakobson, in one of his several brilliant articles on Mayakovsky,• has called this exercise "personal censorship." He points out that Mayakovsky went so far as to attack other poets for his own presumed weakness. "The 10th anniversary of the October Revolution is at hand," Mayakovsky wrote in *Komsomolskaya Pravda* in 1927, admonishing another poet, "and you have caught at someone's braids. Go ahead and love both Mary and her braids, but these are your family affairs, and to us your woman doesn't matter." And again, at an exhibition of his posters and writings which opened three weeks before his death, he pontificated: "Why should I write on Mary's love for Peter instead of considering myself part of that state organ which builds life. The basic goal of the exhibition is . . . to show that the poet is not one who, like a woolly lamb, bleats of lyric-erotic themes, but one who, in our acute class struggle, surrenders his pen to the arsenal of proletarian arms."

Nevertheless, Vladimir's love for Lily and other women had resulted in some remarkable lyrics, among them *I Love* (1922), an anguished declaration of love for Lily; *About This* (1923), his cry of despair at Lily's infidelity; *Letter from Paris to Comrade Kostrov on the Nature of Love* (1928), a direct expression of the rival claims of love and communism on the poet.

The struggle within Mayakovsky between the propagandist and the lyric poet sharpened in the mid-twenties. For one thing, his position as the foremost revolutionary poet was being questioned. Writers who considered themselves ideologically orthodox had begun to carp at him for his experimentalism and his independence. And LEF (Left Front of Literature),

• "Unpublished Mayakovsky," Harvard Library Bulletin, Vol. 9, 1955.

the movement he had helped found along with other futurists, was under fire. LEF's program, like futurism's, was to create bold new forms in the arts which would be worthy of the technological and revolutionary era. Mayakovsky and his colleagues called the realist writers bourgeois, and the so-called proletarian writers official and academic. The LEF magazine published some of the finest works of the period, including Isaac Babel's superb *Red Cavalry*. Lecturing in defense of LEF, Mayakovsky said in 1927: "When Babel came to the capital three years ago with a collection of his short stories, he was received with bayonets. They told him: 'If you saw such things in the Red Cavalry, you should have reported them to the commanding officer instead of putting them into a story.' After that LEF—because LEF does not follow the line of stereotype criticism—published his best stories." • The magazine folded right after the publication of the stories. (Babel was arrested in 1939 and died in prison two years later.)

Mayakovsky was shaken by LEF's failure, and partly to get away from his critics, undertook a long trip through Europe and America in 1925. But the journey only served to agitate him more, for in America he was compelled to alter at least one long-standing conviction, and this was that modernity represented an unmixed blessing for mankind. True, during his first days in New York he marveled at the "austere disposition of bolts and steel" of the Brooklyn Bridge; "construction instead of style" fitted in nicely with the LEF-futurist ideology. But in the long run, America frightened him, as it had frightened many a European during the frantic, booming, money-mad

• *Literaturnoe nasledstvo,* Vol. 65, *"Novoe o Mayakovskom,"* Moscow, 1958.

twenties. Mayakovsky saw New York as a suffocating prison of tunnels, elevateds, elevators, and sinister streets where "the filth is worse than in Minsk. It is extremely dirty in Minsk." Besides, he was personally miserable during his three-month stay in America. He felt desperately homesick as he traveled alone, in the infernal summer heat, to Chicago, Detroit, Pittsburgh, and other unlovely monuments to industrialization. Since he spoke no English, or any other foreign language for that matter, he had only Russian-speaking immigrants for company. Under the circumstances it is astonishing that his account of his journey, *My Discovery of America* (1925-6), contains so many perceptive descriptions, as well as savage caricatures of American life. Most interesting are his conclusions: "The futurism of naked technology with the superficial impressionism of smoke and wires which has the enormous task of revolutionizing the paralyzed, obese, and ancient psyche—this elemental futurism has been definitely confirmed by America. . . . The task of LEF arises before the workers in the field of art; not the hymning of technology but its control in the name of the interests of humanity. Not the aesthetic enjoyment of iron fire escapes but the simple organization of living quarters."

On his way home, he made another discovery: France, which had once seemed the most decadent of capitalist countries, now had a certain charm for him. *My Discovery of America* ends on this note: "In comparison with America's wretched hovels, each inch of land [in France] has been captured by age-long struggle, exhausted by centuries, and used with pharmaceutical minuteness to grow violets or lettuce. But even this despised sort of little house, this little bit of land, this property, even this deliberate clinging for centuries seemed to me now an unbelievable cultural milieu in comparison with the bivouac-type set-up and the self-seeking character of American life." •

Mayakovsky returned to Moscow from this journey in an abject mood. After his loneliness abroad and his disturbing impressions of America and France, he yearned—temporarily, at least—to submit to the familiar certitudes of communism. The result was *Back Home!*, a poem which is at once the most outrageous and the most pathetic expression of Mayakovsky's attraction to dictatorship—outrageous, as he calls upon the Gosplan, a commissar, a factory committee, and Stalin himself to command his work—and pathetic as he explains, "but I,/from poetry's skies,/ plunge into communism,/because/without it/I feel no love." The mood did not last long. Even while writing *Back Home!*, he sensed that his reception in Moscow would be far from reassuring. A first version of the poem ended: "I want to be understood by my country,/but if I fail to be understood—/what then?/ I shall pass through my native land/to one side,/like a shower/of slanting rain."

Back home, the "proletarian" hacks he so despised for their conservatism were gaining power. Mayakovsky's attempt to revive the LEF magazine in 1927 failed almost at once under their assault. By 1928, the RAPP (Association of Proletarian Writers) controlled Soviet literary life; the era of liberalism in the arts was very nearly over. Some of the most independent and original of Soviet intellectuals were now being attacked for their "anarchism," and, more ominously, for their "Trotskyist left deviations." Writers were

• Excerpts from *My Discovery of America* translated by Charles A. Moser.

called upon to be "shock workers" in "art brigades" in the service of the first five-year plan. Stalin, now embarked on the forced collectivization of the peasantry, was preparing the way for the decimation of the intelligentsia.

At this point, Mayakovsky passed into the most genuinely tragic period of his life. During the two years before his suicide he came closest to an awareness of the nature of the society he had once acclaimed. He saw the conflict between the ideals and the reality of communism, between the individual and the collective, between the artist and the bureaucrat. And although this knowledge ultimately proved intolerable, it is to Mayakovsky's honor that, at the last, he chose to confront it in his art.

In 1928 he wrote one of the most devastating satires of communist society in contemporary literature: *The Bedbug* (*Klop*). In the first half of the play, he sees the Russia of 1928 in terms of the Soviet bourgeoisie: the profiteers, the Party fat cats, the proletarian philistines. His villain is Prisypkin, the bedbug-infested, guitar-strumming, vodka-soaked vulgarian who is the proud possessor of a Party card and a proletarian pedigree. In the second half, Mayakovsky foresees the communist millennium. Now, in 1978, the excesses of a Prisypkin are unthinkable. Sex, vodka, tobacco, dancing, and romance are merely items in the lexicon of archaisms. The hero? None other than Prisypkin, who has been resurrected as a zoological curiosity and who begins to look nearly human in this dehumanized world. He is lost, frightened, utterly deprived of love —in short, he is a caricature of his author. To sharpen the resemblance on stage, Mayakovsky took pains to teach the actor who played Prisypkin his own mannerisms.

Roman Jakobson has pointed out that Mayakovsky was making fun of his own youthful hopes in the second part of *The Bedbug*. ● His evidence is arresting. In *150,000,-000* (1919-20) Mayakovsky had prophesied that "in the new world/roses and daydreams once desecrated by poets will blossom,/to gladden/the eyes/of us overgrown children." But when Prisypkin plaintively requests books on roses and daydreams, he is told that "nobody knows anything about what you asked for. Only textbooks on horticulture have anything on roses, and daydreams are dealt with only in medical works—in the section on hypnosis." In *Man* (1916-17) Mayakovsky had cried: "I am for the heart!" Prisypkin wants "something that . . . plucks at my heartstrings." The reply: "Well, here's a book by someone called Mussolini: *Letters from Exile*." In *About This* (1923) Mayakovsky had petitioned a chemist of the "Future Workshop of Human Resurrection" of the thirtieth century: "I have not lived out my earthly span/on earth,/I have not finished loving/.... Resurrect me—/I want to live out my life!/... I'll do anything you want for nothing./ ... Do you/have/zoos?/Let me be a keeper." Prisypkin ends up *inside* the cage, with an armed keeper.

Prisypkin's last lines are an ominous invitation. Momentarily released from his cage, he walks to the footlights and addresses the audience: "Citizens! Brothers! My own people! Darlings! How did you get here? So many of you! . . . Why am I alone in the cage? Darlings, friends, come and join me! Why am I suffering? Citizens!"

But in 1928 Mayakovsky's audience was not ready to recognize his warning. Then, *The Bedbug* ap-

● "New Verse of Mayakovsky," Russian Literary Archive, New York, 1956.

peared to be dealing with periods in time that had no immediacy for the literal-minded. In the first part of the play, Mayakovsky had chosen to identify his repulsive characters with the NEP (New Economic Policy) which had already been supplanted by the first five-year plan. As for the second part, the nature of the Stalinist utopia was as yet beyond the imagination of all but prophets, madmen, and poets. Moreover, *The Bedbug* was first produced in Meyerhold's most constructivist style, then much too avant-garde for a mass audience. In short, the play was not a success. After a three-month run in Moscow, it was performed only rarely, briefly, and usually in abridged form, for twenty-five years.

Nowadays, the Russian audience that has endured the Stalin era is more appreciative of *The Bedbug*. When the authorities permitted a full-scale repertory production in Moscow in 1955, it became a smash hit. Since then it has been staged, with great success, in cities all over the country. Significantly, some of these productions have heightened the immediacy of Prisypkin's plight, perhaps beyond Mayakovsky's intention. In the original production, his cage was a fantasy of glass and string; today it has iron bars and is provided with some familiar furnishings of contemporary Soviet life: the fringed orange lampshade, the fake tapestry hanging, and the ruffled boudoir pillow. The puritans of 1978 who express their repugnance for romance and vodka now do so against a backdrop showing the new University of Moscow building, completed in 1953. In at least one production, Prisypkin has become a tragic hero. When the resurrected Prisypkin has been abandoned in horror by the doctors of the brave new world, the lights in the laboratory dim; a single spotlight illuminates him as he kneels, beating

39

his head on the stage. His cry, *"Odin!"*, *"Alone!"*, howled into the darkness, is surely one of the most hair-raising effects in modern theater. The audience which, only a few moments before, was laughing at Prisypkin's antics, is now frozen in absolute silence. The sense of Prisypkin's last lines is unmistakable to such an audience, but in case anyone should miss the point, the director sends him running past the footlights, down the steps, and into the aisles. "Come and join me!" he cries, just as his keeper collars him and forces him back to his cage with a gun at his head.

Bold as such productions appear in Moscow today, the Meyerhold-Mayakovsky version was a far riskier enterprise as Russia entered the Stalin era. There can hardly be anyone among those who now throng to see *The Bedbug* who does not know the fate of its creators. In 1937 Meyerhold was accused in *Pravda* of consistently producing anti-Soviet plays. He was arrested in 1939 and perished in a concentration camp during the war. Mayakovsky would unquestionably have joined Meyerhold if he had not taken his execution into his own hands.

Yet, Mayakovsky's position was reasonably secure in 1928. The critics did not dare attack *The Bedbug* openly, but Mayakovsky was acutely aware of grumblings behind the scenes. A few days after the first public reading of the play, he published a poem which, he confided to friends, he knew to be a "bomb": *Letter from Paris to Comrade Kostrov on the Nature of Love.* Kostrov, the editor of the magazine *Young Guard*, had commissioned him to write some political articles and poems from Paris, where Mayakovsky spent a month in 1928. But instead of providing the editor with his customary accounts of French decadence, he submitted an ecstatic love poem. Writing from Paris,

40

where he had fallen in love, Mayakovsky suggested that such a man as Kostrov can neither comprehend nor curb the overwhelming force of the poet's passions: "Hurricane,/fire,/water/surge forward, rumbling./Who/can/control this?/Can you?/Try it. . . ."

The poem was, of course, received angrily by the authorities, as was the news of Mayakovsky's Parisian love affair. The girl, as all Moscow now knew, was a worldly White Russian émigrée, "a beauty/all inset in furs and beads." Tatiana Yakovleva had fled from Russia in 1925 to join her uncle, the well-known painter Alexander Yakovlev, in Paris. Greatly admired for her statuesque Russian-style beauty, she moved in a circle of famous and fashionable people, and posed for the fashion pages of *Vogue*. At eighteen, when Mayakovsky first encountered her, she was a dazzling creature, in her furs and beads, and, as he well knew, the most unorthodox partner imaginable for a Soviet citizen of his reputation.

Nevertheless, it appeared that they were exceedingly well-suited; friends remarked that they resembled one another physically and temperamentally. Nearly as tall as Mayakovsky, Tatiana had something like the same powerfully molded features, the same direct, determined manner. Moreover, Mayakovsky was thrilled over her "perfect pitch" for poetry; he recited Pasternak, Esenin and his own verses to her by the hour. Despite their differences in age and background, the intelligent and strong-willed Tatiana could meet Mayakovsky on his own ground. He was, in turn, extraordinarily gentle with her and tried to tone down his ordinarily rough, crude language in her presence. Clearly, he was more wholeheartedly in love than ever before in his life. In Paris he seemed to have found the answer to the question he had posed at twenty-two: "Where shall I find a beloved,/a beloved like me?" •

He wanted, at all costs, to remove Tatiana from her circle of admirers, marry her, and take her back to Moscow with him. In a single night in November 1928, he composed a poem, *Letter to Tatiana Yakovleva,* in which he stated his jealousy and his determination: "We need you in Moscow,/there's a shortage of long-legged people./It's not for you who walked/in snowdrifts and typhus••/with those legs of yours/to surrender them/to the caresses/of oil magnates/at banquets/. . . Come here!/Come to the crossroads/of my large/and clumsy arms./You don't want to?/Well, stay behind and winter here/. . . But—all the same/one day/I'll take you—/you alone—/or together with Paris."

When Mayakovsky returned to Moscow he felt wretched without Tatiana. "To work and to wait for you is my *only* joy," he emphasized in a letter to her, as he completed work on *The Bedbug* and rushed it through production.••• At the end of February 1929, a week after the opening of his play, he fled to Tatiana. By this time, Mayakovsky had learned to love Paris, in company with the ravishing Tatiana. Her smart, luxurious world now had a strong appeal for him. He bought custom-tailored suits for himself and dresses for Lily Brik, to whom he was still morbidly attached. The Parisian salons he frequented with Tatiana made Moscow life seem provincial by comparison. Together, they visited Le Touquet, and Paris

• *To His Beloved Self, the Author Dedicates these Lines* (1916).
•• A reference to Tatiana's rather perilous exit from Russia in 1925.
••• Microfilms of Mayakovsky's letters and telegrams to Tatiana have been deposited in the Houghton Library, Harvard University.

Plage, a resort near Deauville, where he spent days at the roulette tables among Europe's most fashionable people. But by the time his visa had expired at the end of March, he had not succeeded in persuading her to follow him to Moscow; she was quite understandably reluctant to take the risk. Mayakovsky still hoped to bring her around on a subsequent visit, or at least, spend as much time with her in Paris as possible in the future.

His letters and telegrams to Tatiana from Moscow during the summer and fall of 1929 reflect his growing anxiety about their reunion. "I am trying to see you as soon as possible," he wired in May. In June he sent a series of telegrams: "Am very depressed . . . impossibly depressed . . . absolutely depressed . . . yearning for you unprecedentedly . . . yearning for you regularly and recently not even regularly but even more often." By July he was desperate, and suggested that she come as an "engineer" to Russia and settle with him in the desolate Altai region. Finally, in September, when he was scheduled to leave for Paris at last, he wrote: "It is impossible to repeat and enumerate all those sorrows that make me even more taciturn." He had been refused a visa by the authorities. "Only a great, good love could still save me," he had told friends in 1927. Now he was saying, "I am being torn, chopped into pieces; people are being ripped away from me." In December he learned that Tatiana had married a Frenchman.•

The denial of a visa to Mayakovsky was obviously an attempt to break his independence. But even in his grief over the loss of Tatiana, he had the courage

• In connection with this reconstruction of Mayakovsky's last two journeys to Paris, I am greatly indebted to Mrs. Yakovleva, and to Professor Roman Jakobson for the material contained in his articles cited on pp. 33 and 38.

to fight back; his play *The Bathhouse* (*Banya*) was a direct assault on the bureaucracy that was closing in on him. *The Bathhouse*'s main character is the grotesque Pobedonosikov, the director of a huge "co-ordination" service, who is busily engaged in avoiding work. His activities include having his portrait painted to "immortalize the new-style administrator." "How shiny your boots are!" raves the painter. "Makes one feel like licking them! Only Michelangelo had such pure lines. Do you know Michelangelo?" "Angelov, an Armenian?" answers the director.

When Pobedonosikov is taken to see a play in which his own idiocies are represented on stage, he protests: "Your theater pretends to be revolutionary but you irritate . . . how do you say . . . you shake up responsible officials. This is not for the masses; workers and peasants won't understand it, and it's just as well they won't understand it, and it shouldn't be explained to them. What do you mean by making us into actors on the stage? We want to be passive, like . . . how do you say it . . . spectators?"

The cultural bureaucrats had tolerated Mayakovsky's satire of the communist millennium in *The Bedbug*, but they were determined not to let him get away with assailing the present-day regime. After a first reading in February 1930, Glavrepertkom, the theater censorship committee, declared that the play was not acceptable in its present form. Only Mayakovsky's still formidable reputation saved it from being scrapped altogether. After some alterations, it was produced the following month and failed as badly as *The Bedbug*. This time, some of Mayakovsky's enemies were outspoken, both in the press and in public meetings. A few reviews had a sinister ring. The critic and official of RAPP Vladimir Ermilov, for example, insinuated in *Pravda*• that Mayakovsky was playing the game of the Trotskyist opposition. A few days later, Mayakovsky composed a slogan which he had painted on a huge poster and displayed in the Meyerhold Theater: "You can't immediately steam out the swarm of bureaucrats./There wouldn't be enough bathhouses or soap./Besides, the bureaucrats are aided by the pen of critics—/like Ermilov."

Ermilov protested; RAPP ordered that the poster be removed at once. Here the incident ended until Mayakovsky recalled it a month later. A postscript to his suicide note reads: "Tell Ermilov it was a pity he removed the slogan; we should have fought it out."

Always hypersensitive to criticism and stricken by failure, Mayakovsky believed he was now the victim of persecution. In reality, his enemies were more restrained in their criticism than he imagined, or as is generally supposed in the West. Yet his presentiment of tragedy was, as always, uncanny; the purges of the intelligentsia were at hand. Mayakovsky evidently sensed that he would be among the first to be condemned. His last important poem, the unfinished *At the Top of My Voice,* was conceived as a monument to a doomed man—Vladimir Mayakovsky. The poem was clearly inspired by Pushkin who, at the age of thirty-seven, five months before his death, had written: "No hands have wrought my monument; no weeds/ will hide the nation's footpath to its site./Tsar Alexander's column it exceeds/in splendid insubmissive height./••Mayakovsky echoed: "My verse/by labor/ will break the mountain chain of years,/and will

• "On Petty-bourgeois Leftishness in Literature," *Pravda,* March 9, 1930.
•• *Exegi Monumentum* (1836), translated by Vladimir Nabokov, in *Three Russian Poets,* New Directions, New York, 1944.

present itself/ponderous,/crude,/tangible,/as an aqueduct,/by slaves of Rome/constructed,/enters into our days."

Here, in *At the Top of My Voice,* he made a final defense of the purity of his ideals and the quality of his accomplishments in the name of socialism, "above the heads/of a gang of self-seeking/poets and rogues." Here, too, he suggested the cost of these accomplishments: "Agitprop/sticks/in my teeth too/. . . But I/ subdued/myself,/setting my heel/on the throat/of my own song."

Mayakovsky was immensely wearied by the polemics of the last months of his life. He made the effort to debate his critics at public meetings, but his answers to heckling from the floor were often contradictory, even incoherent. After he had made a speech at the House of Komsomol on March 25, the following exchange took place:

QUESTION FROM THE FLOOR: Are you a Party member?
MAYAKOVSKY: No, I'm not.
VOICE: You should be.
MAYAKOVSKY: I don't think so . . . I have acquired a large number of habits which are incompatible with organized work. Perhaps it is a wild prejudice, but I have been carrying on such a bitter struggle, I have been attacked so much. . . . Instead of organized struggle I made anarchic forays because I thought that such a line in literature would converge with the proletarian line. . . . Why the devil am I forced to do things that one doesn't need to do! Habits acquired in the prerevolutionary years are firmly rooted in me. I do not sever myself from the Party and regard myself obliged to carry out all the commands of the Bolshevik Party, even though I do not carry a Party card.●

● Vladimir Mayakovsky, *Complete Works,* Izd. Khudozhestvennoi Literatury, Vol. 10, Moscow, 1939-47.

At the beginning of April, Mayakovsky was taken to the Kremlin hospital for a few days with a breakdown that was diagnosed as nervous exhaustion. After his release, he stated at a writers' meeting that "so much abuse is being flung at me and I'm being accused of so many sins (real and unreal) that I sometimes think that I should go away somewhere for a year or two so as not to listen to so much invective." • On April 10 an acquaintance ran into him in the lobby of the Meyerhold Theater. His account of their meeting is reported in the authoritative Soviet work on Mayakovsky: "He was very gloomy. I started talking to him about how at last there had been an article in *Pravda* giving an objective assessment of *The Bathhouse*. Mayakovsky replied: 'Never mind. It's too late now.' Then I understood him to mean that it didn't matter because the play had already been cursed to pieces." •• Four days later, Mayakovsky was dead.

His suicide note, addressed "to all," reads in part: "Do not blame anyone for my death and please do not gossip. The deceased terribly disliked this sort of thing. Mamma, sisters, and comrades, forgive me—this is not a way out (I do not recommend it to others), but I have none other. Lily—love me. . . . Comrades of VAPP •••—do not think me weak-spirited. Seriously —there was nothing else I could do. Greetings."

What followed was worthy of Mayakovsky's prophecies of the brave new world of 1978. *Literary Gazette* reported that at 8 p.m. on the day of his death the

---

• From the essay "On the Generation Which Squandered Its Poets," by Roman Jakobson, *The Death of Vladimir Mayakovsky*, Petropolis, Berlin, 1931.
•• *Vladimir Mayakovsky: A Literary Chronicle*, by V. Katanyan, Moscow, 1956.
••• The all-union organization of RAPP.

State Institute for the Study of the Brain extracted Mayakovsky's brain; it weighed 1,700 grams as against an average of 1,400, and was put in the Institute's "Pantheon." During the next days, 150,000 people came to view his body as it lay in state at the Club of the Writers' Federation, under a wreath made of hammers, flywheels, and screws which bore the inscription: "An iron wreath to an iron poet." • His obituary in *Pravda* contained a cry of outrage by the ultra-proletarian poet Demyan Bedny: "Monstrous. Incomprehensible. The tragedy of his so unexpected end is heightened by its triviality, which is completely out of tune with the questing and original nature of Mayakovsky. And this ghastly letter before his death which is so ghastly in its triviality—what sort of a justification is this? . . . I cannot explain this except as a sudden mental collapse, a loss of inner orientation, a morbid crisis of personal experience, an acute psychosis." ••

At the funeral, another sort of explanation was provided by members of RAPP, led by the critic Leopold Averbach. The trouble was, they chorused, that Mayakovsky had not become a truly proletarian poet; the dead hand of the past had still been upon him. Said Averbach: "Mayakovsky gave an example of how one should reform oneself and also of how difficult it is to do this. In his last letter Mayakovsky asked his comrades of RAPP not to condemn his act. We do condemn his act . . . but we pay homage to the gigantic creative path which he has traveled." ••• Unfortunately for Averbach and his colleagues, Stalin was to put still another interpretation on Mayakovsky's

• *Literary Gazette,* April 21, 1930.
•• *Pravda,* April 15, 1930.
••• *Literary Gazette,* April 21, 1930.

suicide: he blamed it on them. Some time after the liquidation of RAPP in 1932, it was revealed that Mayakovsky had been driven to his grave by "enemies of the people" in RAPP.•

Nevertheless, the fact of Mayakovsky's suicide still troubled some Party purists. For several years, contributors to *Literary Gazette's* Mayakovsky anniversary numbers suggested that he had not been, after all, a "reinforced-concrete proletarian poet." And although his verse continued to be published in enormous editions, cases of "over-vigilance" were reported in the press. Misguided bureaucrats, for example, had removed his books from children's libraries as "allegedly unsuitable,"•• and the chief of broadcasting for the lower Volga region, a certain Comrade Lemaren (who had recently changed his name to an abbreviation of the trinity Lenin-Marx-Engels) forbade the recitation of Mayakovsky's *Vladimir Ilyich Lenin* because he had doubts as to the poem's political soundness.•••

As the time of the great purges approached, it became increasingly difficult for a good Communist to know what line to take on Mayakovsky—or on any other Soviet intellectual. It appeared that the official critic who denounced a writer on one day might be liquidated the next, along with his victim. Finally, all doubts about Mayakovsky were dispelled by Stalin in 1935, during the period of mass arrests which followed the assassination of Kirov. Banner headlines•••• carried Stalin's message to the Soviet people: "Mayakov-

• This Stalinist myth, which endured in Russia until recently, is evidently at the source of the assumption, widely held abroad, that Mayakovsky died the victim of a campaign of persecution.
•• *Literary Gazette*, July 10, 1930.
••• *Literary Gazette*, February 17, 1933.
•••• *Literary Gazette*, December 9 and 20, 1935.

sky was and remains the best and the most talented poet of our Soviet epoch." Rarely quoted nowadays, but infinitely more meaningful at the time, is the second part of his message: "Indifference to his memory and to his work is a crime." Within days, the Council of People's Commissars reported that they had renamed Moscow's Triumphal Square after Mayakovsky. A new subway station was excavated in his honor. His statues cropped up in Parks of Culture and Rest all over the nation. Commissars and critics began vying with each other in proclaiming the orthodoxy of his political views. His ashes were removed from a mortuary and placed among the graves of Gogol and Stalin's wife, in Moscow's Novo-Devechy Cemetery, where they now rest under a gigantic red-and-black marble monument.

Of Mayakovsky's fate since Stalin's pronouncement, Pasternak has written that he "began to be introduced forcibly, like potatoes under Catherine the Great. This was his second death. He had no hand in it." •

• *An Essay in Autobiography,* Collins and Harvill Press, London, 1959.

SELECTED POETRY

СТИХИ ПОЭМЫ

Я

1

По мостовой
моей души изъезженной
шаги помешанных
вьют жестких фраз пяты.
Где города
повешены
и в петле óблака
застыли
башен
кривые выи —
иду
один рыдать,
что перекрестком
рáспяты
городовые.

2

НЕСКОЛЬКО СЛОВ О МОЕЙ ЖЕНЕ

Морей неведомых далеким пляжем
идет луна —
жена моя.
Моя любовница рыжеволосая.
За экипажем
крикливо тянется толпа созвездий пестрополосая.
Венчается автомобильным гаражем,
целуется газетными киосками,
а шлейфа млечный путь моргающим пажем
украшен мишурными блестками.
А я?

I

1

On the pavement
of my trampled soul
the steps of madmen
weave the prints of rude crude words.
Where cities
hang
and in the noose of cloud
the towers'
crooked spires
congeal—
I go
alone to weep
that crossroads
crucify
policemen.

2

A FEW WORDS ABOUT MY WIFE

Along far beaches of uncharted seas
the moon—
my wife—goes driving.
She's redhaired, my beloved.
Behind her turnout,
a variegated throng of constellations scurries,
screaming.
She weds with a garage,
kisses newspaper kiosks,
while a fluttering-eyed page tinsels her train, the
    Milky Way.
And I?

Несло же, палимому, бровей коромысло
из глаз колодцев студеные ведра.
В шелках озерных ты висла,
янтарной скрипкой пели бедра?
В края, где злоба крыш,
не кинешь блесткой лесни.
В бульварах я тону, тоской песков овеян:
ведь это ж дочь твоя —
моя песня
в чулке ажурном
у кофеен!

3

НЕСКОЛЬКО СЛОВ О МОЕЙ МАМЕ

У меня есть мама на васильковых обоях.
А я гуляю в пестрых павах,
вихрастые ромашки, шагом меряя, мучу.
Заиграет вечер на гобоях ржавых,
подхожу к окошку,
веря,
что увижу опять
севшую
на дом
тучу.
А у мамы больной
пробегают народа шорохи
от кровати до угла пустого.
Мама знает —
это мысли сумасшедшей ворохи
вылезают из-за крыш завода Шустова.
И когда мой лоб, венчанный шляпой фетровой,
окровавит гаснущая рама,

To me, ablaze, the yoke of brows
has lugged fresh pails from deep-eyed wells.
In lacustrine silks you hung,
an amber fiddle chanting in your thighs?
You threw no baited line
into the regions of malignant roofs.
In sands' nostalgia bathed, I drown in boulevards;
for that's your daughter—
my song
in mesh of stocking gliding
by the coffee houses!

3

A FEW WORDS ABOUT MY MAMMA

I have a mamma on blue cornflower wallpaper.
But I pace about in peahen colors,
torturing shaggy camomiles with my measuring stride.
When the evening sounds its rusty oboes,
I walk to the window,
believing
I shall see again
the cloud
reposing
upon the house.
But mamma's sick in bed,
and from it
a rustling of people scurries to an empty corner.
Mamma's aware—
this is the helter-skelter of mad thoughts
crawling from behind the roofs of the Shustov factory.[2]
And when the dimming window-frame
bloodies my forehead, crowned with a felt hat,

я скажу,
раздвинув басом ветра вой:
«Мама.
Если станет жалко мне
вазы вашей муки,
сбитой каблуками облачного танца, —
кто же изласкает золотые руки,
вывеской заломленные у витрин Аванцо?..»

4

НЕСКОЛЬКО СЛОВ ОБО МНЕ САМОМ

Я люблю смотреть, как умирают дети.
Вы прибоя смеха мглистый вал заметили
за тоски хоботом?
А я —
в читальне улиц —
так часто перелистывал гро́ба том.
Полночь
промокшими пальцами щупала
меня
и забитый забор,
и с каплями ливня на лысине купола
скакал сумасшедший собор.
Я вижу, Христос из иконы бежал,
хитона оветренный край
целовала, плача, слякоть.
Кричу кирпичу,
слов исступленных вонзаю кинжал
в неба распухшего мякоть:
«Солнце!
Отец мой!

then I shall speak out,
pushing apart with my bass voice the wind's howl:
"Mamma.
If I should feel sorry
for the vase of your torment,
knocked down by the heels of the cloud dance—
who then would fondle the golden hands,
imploringly twisted on the signboard by the shop-
      windows of Avanzo?" [3]

4

A FEW WORDS ABOUT MYSELF

I love to watch children dying.
Do you note, behind protruding nostalgia,
the shadowy billow of laughter's surf?
But I—
in the reading room of the streets—
have leafed so often through the volume of the coffin.
Midnight
with sodden hands has fingered
me
and the battered paling,
and the crazy cathedral galloped
in drops of downpour upon the cupola's bald pate.
I have seen Christ escape from an icon,
and the slush tearfully kiss
the wind-swept fringe of his tunic.
At bricks I bawl,
thrusting the dagger of desperate words
into the swollen pulp of the sky:
"Sun!
Father mine!

Сжалься хоть ты и не мучай!
Это тобою пролитая кровь моя льется дорогою
дольней.

Это душа моя
клочьями порванной тучи
в выжженном небе
на ржавом кресте колокольни!
Время!
Хоть ты, хромой богомаз,
лик намалюй мой
в божницу уродца века!
Я одинок, как последний глаз
у идущего к слепым человека!»
(1913)

If at least *thou* wouldst have mercy and stop torment-
    ing me!
For my blood thou spilled gushes down this nether
    road.
That is my soul yonder
in tatters of torn cloud
against a burnt-out sky
upon the rusted cross of the belfry!
Time!
You lame icon-painter,
will you at least daub my countenance
and frame it as a freak of this age!
I am as lonely as the only eye
of a man on his way to the blind!'"
(1913)

ОБЛАКО В ШТАНАХ

ТЕТРАПТИХ

Вашу мысль,
мечтающую на размягченном мозгу,
как выжиревший лакей на засаленной кушетке,
буду дразнить об окровавленный сердца лоскут,
досыта изъиздеваюсь, нахальный и едкий.

У меня в душе ни одного седого волоса,
и старческой нежности нет в ней!
Мир огро́мив мощью голоса,
иду — красивый,
двадцатидвухлетний.

Нежные!
Вы любовь на скрипки ложите.
Любовь на литавры ложит грубый.
А себя, как я, вывернуть не можете,
чтобы были одни сплошные губы!

Приходите учиться —
из гостиной батистовая,
чинная чиновница ангельской лиги.

И которая губы спокойно перелистывает,
как кухарка страницы поваренной книги.

Хотите —
буду от мяса бешеный
— и, как небо, меняя тона —
хотите —
буду безукоризненно нежный,
не мужчина, а — облако в штанах!

THE CLOUD IN TROUSERS[1]

A TETRAPTYCH

Your thought,
musing on a sodden brain
like a bloated lackey on a greasy couch,
I'll taunt with a bloody morsel of heart;
and satiate my insolent, caustic contempt.

No gray hairs streak my soul,
no grandfatherly fondness there!
I shake the world with the might of my voice,
and walk—handsome,
twentytwoyearold.

Tender souls!
You play your love on a fiddle,
and the crude club their love on a drum.
But you cannot turn yourselves inside out,
like me, and be just bare lips!

Come and be lessoned—
prim officiates of the angelic league,
lisping in drawing-room cambric.

You, too, who leaf your lips like a cook
turns the pages of a cookery book.

If you wish,
I shall rage on raw meat;
or, as the sky changes its hue,
if you wish,
I shall grow irreproachably tender:
not a man, but a cloud in trousers!

Не верю, что есть цветочная Ницца!
Мною опять славословятся
мужчины, залежанные, как больница,
и женщины, истрепанные, как пословица.

1

Вы думаете, это бредит малярия?

Это было,
было в Одессе.

«Приду в четыре», — сказала Мария.

Восемь.
Девять.
Десять.

Вот и вечер
в ночную жуть
ушел от окон,
хмурый,
декабрый.

В дряхлую спину хохочут и ржут
канделябры.

Меня сейчас узнать не могли бы:
жилистая громадина
стонет,
корчится.
Что может хотеться этакой глыбе?
А глыбе многое хочется!

I deny the existence of blossoming Nice!
Again in song I glorify
men as crumpled as hospital beds,
and women as battered as proverbs.

You think malaria makes me delirious?

It happened.
In Odessa, it happened.

"I'll come at four," Maria promised.[2]

Eight.
Nine.
Ten.

Then the evening
turned its back on the windows
and plunged into grim night,
scowling,
Decemberish.

At my decrepit back
the candelabras guffawed and whinnied.

You would not recognize me now:
a bulging bulk of sinews,
groaning
and writhing.
What can such a clod desire?
Though a clod, many things!

Ведь для себя не важно
и то, что бронзовый,
и то, что сердце — холодной железкою.
Ночью хочется звон свой
спрятать в мягкое,
в женское.

И вот,
громадный,
горблюсь в окне,
плавлю лбом стекло окошечное.
Будет любовь или нет?
Какая —
большая или крошечная?
Откуда большая у тела такого:
должно быть, маленький,
смирный любёночек.
Она шарахается автомобильных гудков.
Любит звоночки коночек.

Еще и еще,
уткнувшись дождю
лицом в его лицо рябое,
жду,
обрызганный громом городского прибоя.

Полночь, с ножом мечась,
догна́ла,
зарезала, —
вон его!

Упал двенадцатый час,
как с плахи голова казненного.

The self does not care
whether one is cast of bronze
or the heart has an iron lining.
At night the self only desires
to steep its clangor in softness,
in woman.

And thus,
enormous,
I stood hunched by the window,
and my brow melted the glass.
What will it be: love or no-love?
And what kind of love:
big or minute?
How could a body like this have a big love?
It should be a teeny-weeny,
humble, little love;
a love that shies at the hooting of cars,
that adores the bells of horse-trams.

Again and again
nuzzling against the rain,
my face pressed against its pitted face,
I wait,
splashed by the city's thundering surf.

Then midnight, amok with a knife,
caught up,
cut him down—
out with him!

The stroke of twelve fell
like a head from a block.

В стеклах дождинки серые
свылись,
гримасу громадили,
как будто воют химеры
Собора Парижской Богоматери.

Проклятая!
Что же, и этого не хватит?
Скоро криком издерется рот.

Слышу:
тихо,
как больной с кровати,
спрыгнул нерв.
И вот, —
сначала прошелся
едва-едва,
потом забегал,
взволнованный,
четкий.
Теперь и он и новые два
мечутся отчаянной чечеткой.

Рухнула штукатурка в нижнем этаже.

Нервы —
большие,
маленькие,
многие! —
скачут бешеные,
и уже
у нервов подкашиваются ноги!

А ночь по комнате тинится и тинится, —
из тины не вытянуться отяжелевшему глазу.

On the windowpanes, gray raindrops
howled together,
piling on a grimace
as though the gargoyles
of Notre Dame were howling.

Damn you!
Isn't that enough?
Screams will soon claw my mouth apart.

Then I heard,
softly,
a nerve leap
like a sick man from his bed.
Then,
barely moving
at first,
it soon scampered about,
agitated,
distinct.
Now, with a couple more,
it darted about in a desperate dance.

The plaster on the ground floor crashed.

Nerves,
big nerves,
tiny nerves,
many nerves!—
galloped madly
till soon
their legs gave way.

But night oozed and oozed through the room—
and the eye, weighed down, could not slither out of
    the slime.

Двери вдруг заляскали,
будто у гостиницы
не попадает зуб нá зуб.

Вошла ты,
резкая, как «нате!»,
муча перчатки замш,
сказала:
«Знаете —
я выхожу замуж».

Что ж, выходите.
Ничего.
Покреплюсь.
Видите — спокоен как!
Как пульс
покойника.

Помните?
Вы говорили:
«Джек Лондон,
деньги,
любовь,
страсть», —
а я одно видел:
вы — Джиоконда,
которую надо украсть!

И украли.

Опять влюбленный выйду в игры,
огнем озаряя бровей зáгиб.
Что же!
И в доме, который выгорел,
иногда живут бездомные бродяги!

The doors suddenly banged ta-ra-bang,
as though the hotel's teeth
chattered.

You swept in abruptly
like "take it or leave it!"
Mauling your suede gloves,
you declared:
"D'you know,
I'm getting married."

All right, marry then.
So what.
I can take it.
As you see, I'm calm!
Like the pulse
of a corpse.

Do you remember
how you used to talk?
"Jack London,
money,
love,
passion."
But I saw one thing only:
you, a Gioconda,[3]
had to be stolen!

And you were stolen.

In love, I shall gamble again,
the arch of my brows ablaze.
What of it!
Homeless tramps often find
shelter in a burnt-out house!

Дра́зните?
«Меньше, чем у нищего копеек,
у вас изумрудов безумий».
Помните!
Погибла Помпея,
когда раздразнили Везувий!

Эй!
Господа!
Любители
святотатств,
преступлений,
боен, —
а самое страшное
видели —
лицо мое,
когда
я
абсолютно спокоен?

И чувствую —
«я»
для меня ма́ло.
Кто-то из меня вырывается упрямо.

Allo!
Кто говорит?
Мама?
Мама!
Ваш сын прекрасно болен!
Мама!
У него пожар сердца.
Скажите сестрам, Люде и Оле, —
ему уже некуда деться.

You're teasing me now?
"You have fewer emeralds of madness
than a beggar has kopecks!"
But remember!
When they teased Vesuvius,
Pompeii perished!

Hey!
Gentlemen!
Amateurs
of sacrilege,
crime,
and carnage,
have you seen
the terror of terrors—
my face
when
I
am absolutely calm?

I feel
my "I"
is much too small for me.
Stubbornly a body pushes out of me.

Hello!
Who's speaking?
Mamma?
Mamma!
Your son is gloriously ill!
Mamma!
His heart is on fire.
Tell his sisters, Lyuda and Olya,
he has no nook to hide in.

Каждое слово,
даже шутка,
которые изрыгает обгорающим ртом он,
выбрасывается, как голая проститутка
из горящего публичного дома.

Люди нюхают —
запахло жареным!
Нагнали каких-то.
Блестящие!
В касках!
Нельзя сапожища!
Скажите пожарным:
на сердце горящее лезут в ласках.
Я сам.
Глаза наслезнённые бочками выкачу.
Дайте о ребра опереться.
Выскочу! Выскочу! Выскочу! Выскочу!
Рухнули.
Не выскочишь из сердца!

На лице обгорающем
из трещины губ
обугленный поцелуишко броситься вырос.

Мама!
Петь не могу.
У церковки сердца занимается клирос!

Обгорелые фигурки слов и чисел
из черепа,
как дети из горящего здания.
Так страх
схватиться за небо
высил
горящие руки «Лузитании».

Each word,
each joke,
which his scorching mouth spews,
jumps like a naked prostitute
from a burning brothel.

People sniff
the smell of burnt flesh!
A brigade of men drive up.
A glittering brigade.
In bright helmets.
But no jackboots here!
Tell the firemen
to climb lovingly when a heart's on fire.
Leave it to me.
I'll pump barrels of tears from my eyes.
I'll brace myself against my ribs.
I'll leap out! Out! Out!
They've collapsed.
But you can't leap out of the heart!

From the cracks of the lips
upon a smoldering face
a cinder of a kiss rises to leap.

Mamma!
I cannot sing.
In the heart's chapel the choir loft catches fire!

The scorched figurines of words and numbers
scurry from the skull
like children from a flaming building.
Thus fear,
in its effort to grasp at the sky,
lifted high
the flaming arms of the *Lusitania*.

Трясущимся людям
в квартирное тихо
стоглазое зарево рвется с пристани.
Крик последний, —
ты хоть
о том, что горю, в столетия выстони!

2

Славьте меня!
Я великим не чета.
Я над всем, что сделано,
ставлю «nihil».

Никогда
ничего не хочу читать.
Книги?
Что книги!

Я раньше думал —
книги делаются так:
пришел поэт,
легко разжал уста,
и сразу запел вдохновенный простак —
пожалуйста!
А оказывается —
прежде чем начнет петься,
долго ходят, размозолев от брожения,
и тихо барахтается в тине сердца
глупая вобла воображения.
Пока выкипячивают, рифмами пиликая,
из любвей и соловьев какое-то варево,
улица корчится безъязыкая —
ей нечем кричать и разговаривать.

Into the calm of an apartment
where people quake,
a hundred-eyed blaze bursts from the docks.
Moan
into the centuries,
if you can, a last scream: I'm on fire!

2

Glorify me!
For me the great are no match.
Upon every achievement
I stamp *nihil*.

I never want
to read anything.
Books?
What are books!

Formerly I believed
books were made like this:
a poet came,
lightly opened his lips,
and the inspired fool burst into song—
if you please!
But it seems,
before they can launch a song,
poets must tramp for days with callused feet,
and the sluggish fish of the imagination
flounders softly in the slush of the heart.
And while, with twittering rhymes, they boil a broth
of loves and nightingales,
the tongueless street merely writhes
for lack of something to shout or say.

Городов вавилонские башни,
возгордясь, возносим снова,
а бог
города на пашни
рушит,
мешая слово.

Улица му́ку молча пёрла.
Крик торчком стоял из глотки.
Топорщились, застрявшие поперек горла,
пухлые taxi и костлявые пролетки.
Грудь испешеходили.
Чахотки площе.

Город дорогу мраком запер.

И когда —
все-таки! —
выхаркнула давку на площадь,
спихнув наступившую на горло паперть,
думалось:
в хо́рах архангелова хорала
бог, ограбленный, идет карать!

А улица присела и заорала:
«Идемте жрать!»

Гримируют городу Круппы и Круппики
грозящих бровей морщь,
а во рту
умерших слов разлагаются трупики,
только два живут, жирея —
«сволочь»

In our pride, we raise up again
the cities' towers of Babel,
but god,[4]
confusing tongues,
grinds
cities to pasture.

In silence the street pushed torment.
A shout stood erect in the gullet.
Wedged in the throat,
bulging taxis and bony cabs bristled.
Pedestrians have trodden my chest
flatter than consumption.

The city has locked the road in gloom.

But when—
nevertheless!—
the street coughed up the crush on the square,
pushing away the portico that was treading on its
    throat,
it looked as if:
in choirs of an archangel's chorale,
god, who had been plundered, was advancing in
    wrath!

But the street, squatting down, bawled:
"Let's go and guzzle!"

Krupps and Krupplets paint[5]
a bristling of menacing brows on the city,
but in the mouth
corpselets of dead words putrefy;
and only two thrive and grow fat:
"swine,"

и еще какое-то,
кажется — «борщ».

Поэты,
размокшие в плаче и всхлипе,
бросились от улицы, ероша космы:
«Как двумя такими выпеть
и барышню,
и любовь,
и цветочек под росами?»

А за поэтами —
уличные тыщи:
студенты,
проститутки,
подрядчики.

Господа!
Остановитесь!
Вы не нищие,
вы не смеете просить подачки!

Нам, здоровенным,
с шагом саженьим,
надо не слушать, а рвать их —
их,
присосавшихся бесплатным приложением
к каждой двуспальной кровати!

Их ли смиренно просить:
«Помоги мне!»
Молить о гимне,
об оратории!
Мы сами творцы в горящем гимне —
шуме фабрики и лаборатории.

and another besides,
apparently—"borsch."

Poets,
soaked in plaints and sobs,
break from the street, rumpling their matted hair
over: "How with two such words celebrate
a young lady
and love
and a floweret under the dew?"

In the poets' wake
thousands of street folk:
students,
prostitutes,
salesmen.

Gentlemen!
Stop!
You are no beggars;
how dare you beg for alms!

We in our vigor,
whose stride measures yards,
must not listen, but tear them apart—
them,
glued like a special supplement
to each double bed!

Are we to ask them humbly:
"Assist me!"
Implore for a hymn
or an oratorio!
We ourselves are creators within a burning hymn—
the hum of mills and laboratories.

Что мне до Фауста,
феерией ракет
скользящего с Мефистофолем в небесном паркете!
Я знаю —
гвоздь у меня в сапоге
кошмарней, чем фантазия у Гете!

Я,
златоустейший,
чье каждое слово
душу новородит,
именинит тело,
говорю вам:
мельчайшая пылинка живого
ценнее всего, что я сделаю и сделал!

Слушайте!
Проповедует,
мечась и стеня,
сегодняшнего дня крикогубый Заратустра!
Мы
с лицом, как заспанная простыня,
с губами, обвисшими, как люстра,
мы,
каторжане города-лепрозория,
где золото и грязь изъязвили проказу, —
мы чище венецианского лазорья,
морями и солнцами омытого сразу!

Плевать, что нет
у Гомеров и Овидиев
людей, как мы,
от копоти в оспе.
Я знаю —
солнце померкло б, увидев
наших душ золотые россыпи!

What is Faust to me,
in a fairy splash of rockets
gliding with Mephistopheles on the celestial parquet!
I know—
a nail in my boot
is more nightmarish than Goethe's fantasy!

I,
the most golden-mouthed,[6]
whose every word
gives a new birthday to the soul,
gives a name-day to the body,
I adjure you:
the minutest living speck
is worth more than what I'll do or did!

Listen!
It is today's brazen-lipped Zarathustra
who preaches,
dashing about and groaning!
We,
our face like a crumpled sheet,
our lips pendulant like a chandelier;
we,
the convicts of the City Leprous,
where gold and filth spawned lepers' sores,
we are purer than the azure of Venice,
washed by both the sea and the sun!

I spit on the fact
that neither Homer nor Ovid
invented characters like us,
pock-marked with soot.
I know
the sun would dim, on seeing
the gold fields of our souls!

Жилы и мускулы — молитв верней.
Нам ли вымаливать милостей времени!
Мы —
каждый —
держим в своей пятерне
миров приводные ремни!

Это взвело на Голгофы аудиторий
Петрограда, Москвы, Одессы, Киева,
и не было ни одного,
который
не кричал бы:
«Распни,
распни его!»
Но мне —
люди,
и те, что обидели —
вы мне всего дороже и ближе.

Видели,
как собака бьющую руку лижет?!

Я,
обсмеянный у сегодняшнего племени,
как длинный
скабрезный анекдот,
вижу идущего через горы времени,
которого не видит никто.

Где глаз людей обрывается куцый,
главой голодных орд,
в терновом венце революций
грядет шестнадцатый год.

А я у вас — его предтеча;

Sinews and muscles are surer than prayers.
Must we implore the charity of the times!
We—
each one of us—
hold in our fists
the driving belts of the worlds!

This led to my Golgothas in the halls
of Petrograd, Moscow, Odessa, and Kiev,[7]
where not a man
but
shouted:
"Crucify,
crucify him!"
But for me—
all of you people,
even those that harmed me—
you are dearer, more precious than anything.

Have you seen
a dog lick the hand that thrashed it?!

I,
mocked by my contemporaries
like a prolonged
dirty joke,
I perceive whom no one sees,
crossing the mountains of time.

Where men's eyes stop short,
there, at the head of hungry hordes,
the year 1916 cometh
in the thorny crown of revolutions.

In your midst, his precursor,[8]

я — где боль, везде;
на каждой капле слёзовой течи
ра́спял себя на кресте.
Уже ничего простить нельзя.
Я выжег души, где нежность растили.
Это труднее, чем взять
тысячу тысяч Бастилий!

И когда,
приход его
мятежом оглашая,
выйдете к спасителю —
вам я
душу вытащу,
растопчу,
чтоб большая! —
и окровавленную дам, как знамя.

3

Ах, зачем это,
откуда это
в светлое весело
грязных кулачищ замах!

Пришла
и голову отчаянием занавесила
мысль о сумасшедших домах.

И —
как в гибель дредноута
от душащих спазм
бросаются в разинутый люк —
сквозь свой

I am where pain is—everywhere;
on each drop of the tear-flow
I have nailed myself on the cross.
Nothing is left to forgive.
I've cauterized the souls where tenderness was bred.
It was harder than taking
a thousand thousand Bastilles!

And when,
with rebellion
his advent announcing,
you step to meet the saviour—
then I
shall root up my soul;
I'll trample it hard
till it spread
in blood; and I offer you this as a banner.

3

Ah, wherefrom this,
how explain this
brandishing of dirty fists
at bright joy!

She came,
and thoughts of a madhouse
curtained my head in despair.

And—
as a dreadnought founders
and men in choking spasms
dive out of an open hatch—
so Burlyuk, panic-stricken,

до крика разодранный глаз
лез, обезумев, Бурлюк.
Почти окровавив исслезенные веки,
вылез,
встал,
пошел
и с нежностью, неожиданной в жирном
                                    человеке,
взял и сказал:
«Хорошо!»

Хорошо, когда в желтую кофту
душа от осмотров укутана!
Хорошо,
когда брошенный в зубы эшафоту,
крикнуть:
«Пейте какао Ван-Гутена!»

И эту секунду,
бенгальскую
громкую,
я ни на что б не выменял,
я ни на...

А из сигарного дыма
ликерною рюмкой
вытягивалось пропитое лицо Северянина.

Как вы смеете называться поэтом
и, серенький, чирикать, как перепел!
Сегодня
надо
кастетом
кроиться миру в черепе!

Вы,

crawled
through the screaming gash of his eye.[9]
Almost bloodying his teary eyelids,
he crawled out,
rose,
walked,
and, with tenderness unexpected in one so obese,
announced:
"It's fine!"

It's fine, when a yellow shirt[10]
shields the soul from investigation!
It's fine,
when thrown at the gibbet's teeth,
to shout:
"Drink Van Houten's Cocoa!"

That instant
crackling
like a Bengal light,
I would not exchange for anything,
not for any . . .

Out of the cigar smoke,
Severyanin's drink-sodden face lurched forward [11]
like a liqueur glass.

How dare you call yourself a poet,
and twitter grayly like a quail!
This day
brass knuckles
must
split the world inside the skull!

You,

обеспокоенные мыслью одной —
«изящно пляшу ли», —
смотрите, как развлекаюсь
я —
площадной
сутенер и карточный шулер!

От вас,
которые влюбленностью мокли,
от которых
в столетия слеза лилась,
уйду я,
солнце моноклем
вставлю в широко растопыренный глаз.

Невероятно себя нарядив,
пойду по земле,
чтоб нравился и жегся,
а впереди
на цепочке Наполеона поведу, как мопса.

Вся земля поляжет женщиной,
заерзает мясами, хотя отдаться;
вещи оживут —
губы вещины
засюсюкают:
«цаца, цаца, цаца!»

Вдруг
и тучи
и облачное прочее
подняло на небе невероятную качку,
как будто расходятся белые рабочие,
небу объявив озлобленную стачку.

who are supremely worried by the thought:
"Am I an elegant dancer?"
Look at my way of enjoying life—
I—
a common
pimp and cardsharp!

On you,
steeped in love,
who watered
the centuries with tears,
I'll turn my back, fixing
the sun like a monocle
into my gaping eye.

Donning fantastic finery,
I'll strut the earth
to please and scorch;
and Napoleon
will precede me, like a pug, on a leash.

The earth, like a woman, will flop on her back,
a mass of quivering flesh, ready to yield;
things will come to life—
and their lips
will lisp and lisp:
"Yum-yum-yum!"

Suddenly,
the clouds
and other cloudy things in the sky
will roll and pitch madly
as if workers in white went their way
after declaring a bitter strike against the sky.

Гром из-за тучи, зверея, вылез,
громадные ноздри задорно высморкал,
и небье лицо секунду кривилось
суровой гримасой железного Бисмарка.

И кто-то,
запутавшись в облачных путах,
вытянул руки к кафе —
и будто по-женски,
и нежный как будто,
и будто бы пушки лафет.

Вы думаете —
это солнце нежненько
треплет по щечке кафе?
Это опять расстрелять мятежников
грядет генерал Галифе!

Выньте, гулящие, руки из брюк —
берите камень, нож или бомбу,
а если у которого нету рук —
пришел чтоб и бился лбом бы!

Идите, голодненькие,
потненькие,
покорненькие,
закисшие в блохастом грязненьке!

Идите!
Понедельники и вторники
окрасим кровью в праздники!
Пускай земле под ножами припомнится,
кого хотела опошлить!
Земле,
обжиревшей, как любовница,
которую вылюбил Ротшильд!

More savagely, thunder strode from a cloud,
friskily snorting from enormous nostrils;
and, for a second, the sky's face was twisted
in the Iron Chancellor's grim grimace.[12]

And someone,
entangled in a cloudy mesh,
held out his hands to a café;
and it looked somehow feminine,
and tender somehow,
and somehow like a gun carriage.

You believe
the sun was tenderly
patting the cheeks of the café?
No, it's General Galliffet,[13]
advancing again to mow down the rebels!

Strollers, hands from your pockets—
pick a stone, knife, or bomb;
and if any of you have no arms,
come and fight with your forehead!

Forward, famished ones,
sweating ones,
servile ones,
mildewed in flea-ridden dirt!

Forward!
Painting Mondays and Tuesdays in blood,
we shall turn them into holidays.
Let the earth, at knife's point, remember
whom it wished to debase!
The earth,
bulging like a mistress
whom Rothschild had overfondled!

Чтоб флаги трепались в горячке пальбы,
как у каждого порядочного праздника —
выше вздымайте, фонарные столбы,
окровавленные туши лабазников.

Изругивался,
вымаливался,
резал,
лез за кем-то
вгрызаться в бока.

На небе, красный, как марсельеза,
вздрагивал, околевая, закат.

Уже сумасшествие.

Ничего не будет.

Ночь придет,
перекусит
и съест.

Видите —
небо опять иудит
пригоршнью обрызганных предательством
звезд?
Пришла.
Пирует Мамаем,
задом на город насев.
Эту ночь глазами не проломаем,
черную, как Азеф!

Ежусь, зашвырнувшись в трактирные углы,
вином обливаю душу и скатерть
и вижу:
в углу — глаза круглы, —

That flags may flutter in a fever of gunfire
as on every important holiday—
will you, the street lamps, hoist high up
the battered carcasses of traders.

I swore,
pleaded,
stabbed,
fought to fasten
my teeth into somebody's flesh,

In the sky, red as the Marseillaise,
the sunset shuddered at its last gasp.

It's madness.

Nothing at all will remain.

Night will arrive,
bite in two,
and gobble you up.

Look—
is the sky playing Judas again
with a handful of treachery-spattered stars?
Night came.
Feasted like Mamai,[14]
squatting with its rump on the city.
Our eyes cannot break this night,
black as Azef![15]

I huddle, slumped in corners of saloons;
with vodka drenching my soul and the cloth,
I notice
in one corner—rounded eyes:

глазами в сердце въелась богоматерь.
Чего одаривать по шаблону намалеванному
сиянием трактирную ораву!
Видишь — опять
голгофнику оплеванному
предпочитают Варавву?

Может быть, нарочно я
в человечьем месѝве
лицом никого не новей.
Я,
может быть,
самый красивый
из всех твоих сыновей.

Дай им,
заплесневшим в радости,
скорой смерти времени,
чтоб стали дети, должные подрасти,
мальчики — отцы,
девочки — забеременели.

И новым рожденным дай обрасти
пытливой сединой волхвов,
и придут они —
и будут детей крестить
именами моих стихов.

Я, воспевающий машину и Англию,
может быть, просто,
в самом обыкновенном евангелии
тринадцатый апостол.

И когда мой голос

the madonna's, which bite into the heart.
Why bestow such radiance of painted form
upon the horde infesting a saloon!
Don't you see! They spit
on the man of Golgotha again,
preferring Barabbas.

Deliberately, perhaps,
I show no newer face
amid this human mash.
I,
perhaps,
am the handsomest
of your sons.

Give them,
who are moldy with joy,
a time of quick death,
that children may grow,
boys into fathers,
girls—big with child.

And may new born babes
grow the gray hair of the magi—
and they will come anon
to baptize the infants
with the names of my poems.

I, who praised the machine and England,
I am perhaps quite simply
the thirteenth apostle
in an ordinary gospel.

And whenever my voice

похабно ухает —
от часа к часу,
целые сутки,
может быть, Йисус Христос нюхает
моей души незабудки.

4

Мария! Мария! Мария!
Пусти, Мария!
Я не могу на улицах!
Не хочешь?
Ждешь,
как щеки провалятся ямкою,
попробованный всеми,
пресный,
я приду,
и беззубо прошамкаю,
что сегодня я
«удивительно честный».

Мария,
видишь —
я уже начал сутулиться.

В улицах
люди жир продырявят в четыреэтажных зобах,
высунут глазки,
потертые в сорокгодовой таске, —
перехихикиваться,
что у меня в зубах
— опять! —
черствая булка вчерашней ласки.

rumbles bawdily—
then, from hour to hour,
around the clock,
Jesus Christ may be sniffing
the forget-me-nots of my soul.

4

Maria! Maria! Maria! [16]
Let me in, Maria!
I can't suffer the streets!
You won't?
You'd rather wait
until my cheeks cave in,
until, pawed by everyone,
I arrive,
stale,
toothlessly mumbling
that today I am
"amazingly honest."

Maria,
as you see—
my shoulders droop.

In the streets
men will prick the blubber of four-story craws,
thrust out their little eyes,
worn in forty years of wear and tear—
to snigger
at my champing
again!—
on the hard crust of yesterday's caress.

Дождь обрыдал тротуары,
лужами сжатый жулик,
мокрый, лижет улиц забитый булыжником труп,
а на седых ресницах —
да! —
на ресницах морозных сосулек
слезы из глаз —
да! —
из опущенных глаз водосточных труб.

Всех пешеходов морда дождя обсосала,
а в экипажах лощился за жирным атлетом атлет:
лопались люди,
проевшись насквозь,
и сочилось сквозь трещины сало,
мутной рекой с экипажей стекала
вместе с иссосанной булкой
жевотина старых котлет.

Мария!
Как в зажиревшее ухо втиснуть им тихое слово?
Птица
побирается песней,
поет,
голодна и звонка,
а я человек, Мария,
простой,
выхарканный чахоточной ночью в грязную руку
                                        Пресни.

Мария, хочешь такого?
Пусти, Мария!
Судорогой пальцев зажму я железное горло звонка!

Rain has drowned the sidewalks in sobs;
the puddle-prisoned rogue,
all drenched, licks the corpse of the streets by cobbles
    clobbered,
but on his grizzled eyelashes—
yes!—
on the eyelashes of frosted icicles
tears gush from his eyes—
yes!—
from the drooping eyes of the drainpipes.

The rain's snout licked all pedestrians;
but fleshy athletes, all gleaming, passed by in carriages;
people burst asunder,
gorged to the marrow,
and grease dripped through the cracks;
and the cud of old ground meat,
together with the pulp of chewed bread,
dribbled down in a turbid stream from the carriages.

Maria!
How stuff a gentle word into their fat-bulged ears?
A bird
sings
for alms,
hungry and resonant.
But I am a man, Maria,
a simple man,
coughed up by consumptive night on the dirty hand
    of the Presnya.[17]

Maria, do you want such a man?
Let me in, Maria!
With shuddering fingers I shall grip the doorbell's
    iron throat!

99

Мария!

Звереют улиц выгоны.
На шее ссадиной пальцы давки.

Открой!

Больно!

Видишь — натыканы
в глаза из дамских шляп булавки!

Пустила.

Детка!
Не бойся,
что у меня на шее воловьей
потноживотые женщины мокрой горою сидят, —
это сквозь жизнь я тащу
миллионы огромных чистых любовей
и миллион миллионов маленьких грязных любят.
Не бойся,
что снова,
в измены ненастье,
прильну я к тысячам хорошеньких лиц, —
«любящие Маяковского!» —
да ведь это ж династия
на сердце сумасшедшего восшедших цариц.

Мария, ближе!

В раздетом бесстыдстве,
в боящейся дрожи ли,
но дай твоих губ неисцветшую прелесть:
я с сердцем ни разу до мая не дожили,

Maria!

The paddocks of the streets run wild.
The fingers of the mob mark my neck.

Open up!

I'm hurt!

Look—my eyes are stuck
with ladies' hatpins!

You've let me in.

Darling!
Don't be alarmed
if a mountain of women with sweating bellies
squats on my bovine shoulders—
through life I drag
millions of vast pure loves
and a million million of foul little lovekins.
Don't be afraid
if once again
in the inclemency of betrayal,
I'll cling to thousands of pretty faces—
"that love Mayakovsky!"—
for this is the dynasty
of queens who have ascended the heart of a madman.

Maria, come closer!

Whether in unclothed shame
or shudders of apprehension,
do yield me the unwithered beauty of your lips:
my heart and I have never got as far as May,

а в прожитой жизни
лишь сотый апрель есть.

Мария!
Поэт сонеты поет Тиане,
а я —
весь из мяса,
человек весь —
тело твое просто прошу,
как просят христиане —
«хлеб наш насущный
даждь нам днесь».

Мария — дай!

Мария!
Имя твое я боюсь забыть,
как поэт боится забыть
какое-то
в муках ночей рожденное слово,
величием равное богу.

Тело твое
я буду беречь и любить,
как солдат,
обрубленный войною,
ненужный,
ничей,
бережет свою единственную ногу.

Мария —
не хочешь?
Не хочешь!

Ха!

and in my expended life
there is only a hundredth April.

Maria!
The poet sings sonnets to Tiana,[18]
but I
am all flesh,
a man every bit—
I simply ask for your body
as Christians pray:
"Give us this day
our daily bread!"

Maria—give!

Maria!
I fear to forget your name
as a poet fears to forget
some word
sprung in the torment of the night,
mighty as god himself.

Your body
I shall cherish and love
as a soldier,
amputated by war,
unwanted
and friendless,
cherishes his last remaining leg.

Maria—
you won't have me?
You won't have me!

Ha!

Значит — опять
темно и понуро
сердце возьму,
слезами окапав,
нести,
как собака,
которая в конуру
несет
перееханную поездом лапу.

Кровью сердца дорогу радую,
липнет цветами у пыли кителя.
Тысячу раз опляшет Иродиадой
солнце землю —
голову Крестителя.

И когда мое количество лет
выпляшет до конца —
миллионом кровинок устелется след
к дому моего отца.

Вылезу
грязный (от ночевок в канавах),
стану бок о бок,
наклонюсь
и скажу ему на ухо:

— Послушайте, господин бог!
Как вам не скушно
в облачный кисель
ежедневно обмакивать раздобревшие глаза?
Давайте — знаете —
устроимте карусель
на дереве изучения добра и зла!

Then once again,
darkly and dully,
my heart I shall take,
with tears besprinkled,
and carry it,
like a dog
carries
to its kennel
a paw which a train ran over.

With the heart's blood I gladden the road,
and flowering it sticks to the dusty tunic.
The sun, like Salome,
will dance a thousand times
round the earth—the Baptist's head.

And when my quantity of years
has finished its dance,
a million bloodstains will lie spread
on the path to my father's house.

I shall clamber out
filthy (from sleeping in ditches);
I'll stand at his side
and, bending,
shall speak in his ear:

"Listen, mister god!
Isn't it tedious
to dip your puffy eyes
every day into a jelly of cloud?
Let us—why not—
start a merry-go-round
on the tree of what is good and evil!

Вездесущий, ты будешь в каждом шкапу,
и вина такие расставим по́ столу,
чтоб захотелось пройтись в ки-ка-пу
хмурому Петру Апостолу.
А в рае опять поселим Евочек:
прикажи, —
сегодня ночью ж
со всех бульваров красивейших девочек
я натащу тебе.

Хочешь?

Не хочешь?

Мотаешь головою, кудластый?
Супишь седую бровь?
Ты думаешь —
этот,
за тобою, крыластый,
знает, что такое любовь?

Я тоже ангел, я был им —
сахарным барашком выглядывал в глаз,
но больше не хочу дарить кобылам
из севрской му́ки изваянных ваз.
Всемогущий, ты выдумал пару рук,
сделал,
что у каждого есть голова, —
отчего ты не выдумал,
чтоб было без мук
целовать, целовать, целовать?!

Я думал — ты всесильный божище,
а ты недоучка, крохотный божик.
Видишь, я нагибаюсь,

Omnipresent, you will be in each cupboard,
and with such wines we'll grace the table
that even frowning Apostle Peter
will want to step out in the ki-ka-pou.[19]
In Eden again we'll lodge little Eves:
command—
and this very night, for you,
from the boulevards, I'll round up
all the most beautiful girls.

Would you like that?

You would not?

You shake your head, curlylocks?
You're frowning, gray brows?
You believe
this
creature with wings behind you
knows what love is?

I too am an angel; I was one—
with a sugar lamb's eye I gazed;
but I'll give no more presents to mares
of ornamental vases made of tortured Sèvres.
Almighty, you concocted a pair of hands,
arranged
for everyone to have a head;
but why didn't you see to it
that one could without torture
kiss, and kiss and kiss?!

I thought you a great big god almighty,
but you're a dunce, a minute little godlet.
Watch me stoop

из-за голенища
достаю сапожный ножик.

Крыластые прохвосты!
Жмитесь в раю!
Ерошьте перышки в испуганной тряске!
Я тебя, пропахшего ладаном, раскрою
отсюда до Аляски!

Пустите!

Меня не остановите.
Вру я,
в праве ли,
но я не могу быть спокойней.
Смотрите —
звезды опять обезглавили
и небо окровавили бойней!

Эй, вы!
Небо!
Снимите шляпу!
Я иду!

Глухо.

Вселенная спит,
положив на лапу
с клещами звезд огромное ухо.
(1914—1915)

and reach for a shoemaker's knife
in my boot.

Swindlers with wings,
huddle in heaven!
Ruffle your feathers in shuddering flight!
I'll rip you, reeking of incense,
wide open from here to Alaska!

Let me in!

You can't stop me.
I may be wrong
or right,
but I'm as calm as can be.
Look—
again they've beheaded the stars,
and the sky is bloodied with carnage!

Hey, you!
Heaven!
Off with your hat!
I am coming!

Not a sound.

The universe sleeps,
its huge paw curled
upon a star-infested ear.
(1914-1915)

ФЛЕЙТА—ПОЗВОНОЧНИК

ПРОЛОГ

За всех вас,
которые нравились или нравятся,
хранимых иконами у души в пещере,
как чашу вина в застольной здравице,
подъемлю стихами наполненный череп.

Все чаще думаю —
не поставить ли лучше
точку пули в своем конце.
Сегодня я
на всякий случай
даю прощальный концерт.

Память!
Собери у мозга в зале
любимых неисчерпаемые очереди.
Смех из глаз в глаза лей.
Былыми свадьбами ночь ряди.
Из тела в тело веселье лейте.
Пусть не забудется ночь никем.
Я сегодня буду играть на флейте.
На собственном позвоночнике.

1

Версты улиц взмахами шагов мну.
Куда уйду я, этот ад тая!
Какому небесному Гофману
выдумалась ты, проклятая?!

THE BACKBONE FLUTE[1]

PROLOGUE

For all of you,
who once pleased or still may please,
guarded by icons in the catacomb of the soul,
I shall raise, like a goblet of wine
at a festive board, a skull brimful of verse.

More and more often I think:
it might be far better for me
to punctuate my end with a bullet.
This very day,
just in case,
I'm staging my final performance.

Memory!
Gather into the hall from my brain
the inexhaustible ranks of my loves.
Pour laughter from eye to eye.
Festoon the night with weddings past.
Pour out joy from body to body.
Let no one forget this night.
On this occasion I shall play the flute.
Play on my own backbone.

1

With far-flung steps I crumple miles of streets.
Where shall I go, hiding within me hell?
Accursed woman, what heavenly Hoffmann[2]
has created you in his fancy?!

Буре веселья улицы у́зки.
Праздник нарядных черпал и че́рпал.
Думаю.
Мысли, крови сгустки,
больные и запекшиеся, лезут из черепа.

Мне,
чудотворцу всего, что празднично,
самому на праздник выйти не с кем.
Возьму сейчас и грохнусь навзничь
и голову вымозжу каменным Невским!
Вот я богохулил.
Орал, что бога нет,
а бог такую из пекловых глубин,
что перед ней гора заволнуется и дрогнет,
вывел и велел:
люби!

Бог доволен.
Под небом в круче
измученный человек одичал и вымер.
Бог потирает ладони ручек.
Думает бог:
погоди, Владимир!
Это ему, ему же,
чтоб не догадался, кто́ ты,
выдумалось дать тебе настоящего мужа
и на рояль положить человечьи ноты.
Если вдруг подкрасться к двери спа́ленной,
перекрестить над вами стёганье одеялово,
знаю —
запахнет шерстью па́ленной,
и серой издымится мясо дьявола.

The streets are too narrow for the storm of joy.
The holiday poured and poured out people in Sunday
    best.
I thought.
Thoughts, sick and coagulated
clots of blood, crawled from my skull.

I,
miracle-worker of all that is festive,
have no companion to share this festivity.
Now I'll go and dive,
dashing my brains on the stones of the Nevsky! [3]
I have blasphemed.
Shouted that there is no god,
but out of the infernal depths
god plucked a woman before whom the mountain
    will tremble and shudder;
he brought her forth and commanded:
love her!

God is content.
On a crag under the sky, [4]
a suffering man has turned beast and perished.
God rubs his palms.
God thinks:
just you wait, Vladimir!
So you might not guess who she was,
it was he, he indeed,
who thought of giving her a real husband
and of placing human notes on the piano
If one suddenly tiptoed to the bedroom door
and blessed the quilted cover above you,
I know
there would be a smell of scorching wool,
and the devil's flesh would rise in sulphurous fumes.

А я вместо этого до утра раннего
в ужасе, что тебя любить увели,
метался
и крики в строчки выгранивал,
уже наполовину сумасшедший ювелир.
В карты б играть!
В вино
выполоскать горло сердцу изоханному.

Не надо тебя!
Не хочу!
Все равно
я знаю,
я скоро сдохну.

Если правда, что есть ты,
боже,
боже мой,
если звезд ковер тобою выткан,
если этой боли,
ежедневно множимой,
тобой ниспослана, господи, пытка,
судейскую цепь надень.
Жди моего визита.
Я аккуратный,
не замедлю ни на день.
Слушай,
Всевышний инквизитор!

Рот зажму.
Крик ни один им
не выпущу из искусанных губ я.
Привяжи меня к кометам, как к хвостам лоша-
дным,
и вымчи,

Instead, until early morning,
in horror that you were taken away to be loved,
I rushed about,
faceting my cries into verse,
a diamond-cutter on the verge of madness.
Oh, for a pack of cards!
Oh, for wine
to gargle a sighed-out heart.

I don't need you!
I don't want you!
In any case,
I know
I shall soon croak!

If it is true you exist,
god,
my god,
if the stars' carpet is your weave,
if, of this daily
multiplied pain,
you have imposed the ordeal, o lord;
then wear the chain of a judge.
Wait for my visit.
I am punctual
and shall not delay a day.
Listen,
All-highest inquisitor!

I'll clamp my mouth.
No cry
shall escape my hard-bitten lips.
Bind me to the comets as to horses' tails,
and gallop me away,

рвя о звездные зубья.
Или вот что:
когда душа моя выселится,
выйдет на суд твой,
выхмурясь тупенько,
ты,
Млечный Путь перекинув виселицей,
возьми и вздерни меня, преступника.
Делай, что́ хочешь.
Хочешь, четвертуй.
Я сам тебе, праведный, руки вымою.
Только —
слышишь! —
убери проклятую ту,
которую сделал моей любимою!

Версты улиц взмахами шагов мну.
Куда я денусь, этот ад тая!
Какому небесному Гофману
выдумалась ты, проклятая?

2

И небо,
в дымах забывшее, что голубо́,
и тучи, ободранные беженцы точно,
вызарю в мою последнюю любовь,
яркую, как румянец у чахоточного.

Радостью покрою рев
скопа
забывших о доме и уюте.
Люди,
слушайте!

tearing at the stars' bit.
Or this perhaps:
when my soul leaves its lodging
and presents itself to your judgment,
then, frowning dully,
you,
throwing a gibbet astride the Milky Way,
seize me and string me up, a criminal.
Do what you will.
Quarter me if you will.
I myself will wash your hands clean.
But do this—
do you hear!—
remove that cursed woman
whom you have made my beloved!

With far-flung steps I crumple miles of streets.
Where shall I go, hiding within me hell?
Accursed woman, what heavenly Hoffmann
has created you in his fancy?!

2

To both the sky,
in smoke oblivious it was blue,
and the clouds resembling ragged refugees,
I shall bring the dawn of my ultimate love,
bright as a consumptive's flush.

With rejoicing I shall blanket the roar
of the assemblage,
oblivious of comfort and home.
Men,
listen to me!

Вылезьте из окопов.
После довоюете.

Даже если,
от крови качающийся, как Бахус,
пьяный бой идет —
слова любви и тогда не ветхи.
Милые немцы!
Я знаю,
на губах у вас
гётевская Гретхен.
Француз,
улыбаясь, на штыке мрет,
с улыбкой разбивается подстреленный авиатор,
если вспомнят
в поцелуе рот
твой, Травиата.

Но мне не до розовой мякоти,
которую столетия выжуют.
Сегодня к новым ногам лягте!
Тебя пою,
накрашенную,
рыжую.

Может быть, от дней этих,
жутких, как штыков острия,
когда столетия выбелят бороду,
останемся только
ты
и я,
бросающийся за тобой от города к городу.

Будешь за́ море отдана,
спрячешься у ночи в норе —
я в тебя вцелую сквозь туманы Лондона
огненные губы фонарей.

Crawl out of those trenches:
you will fight it out another day.

Even if,
rolling in blood like Bacchus,
a drunken battle rages at its height—
even then words of love are not outmoded.
Dear Germans!
I know
Goethe's Gretchen
springs to your lips.
The Frenchman
dies smiling on a bayonet;
an airman crashes down with a smile;
when they remember
your kissing mouth,
Traviata.

But I'm in no mood for the rosy pulp
the centuries have chewed.
This day let me embrace new feet!
You I shall sing,
redhead
with rouged lips.

Perhaps, outliving these times
as harrowing as bayonets' steel,
in centuries with whitened beards
we alone shall remain:
you
and I,
chasing after you from city to city.

You shall be wedded beyond the sea,
and shall bide in night's lair—
in a London fog I'll imprint
on you the fiery lips of the street lamps.

В зное пустыни вытянешь караваны,
где львы начеку, —
тебе
под пылью, ветром рваной,
положу Сахарой горящую щеку.

Улыбку в губы вложишь,
смотришь —
тореадор хорош как!
И вдруг я
ревность метну в ложи
мрущим глазом быка.

Вынесешь на́ мост шаг рассеянный —
думать,
хорошо внизу бы.
Это я
под мостом разлился Сеной,
зову,
скалю гнилые зубы.

С другим зажгешь в огне рысаков
Стрелку или Сокольники.
Это я, взобравшись туда высоко,
луной томлю, ждущий и голенький.

Сильный,
понадоблюсь им я —
велят:
себя на войне убей!
Последним будет
твое имя,
запекшееся на выдранной ядром губе.

Короной кончу?
Святой Еленой?

In a sultry desert, where lions are alert,
you will unfurl your caravans—
upon you,
beneath the wind-torn sands,
I'll place my cheek burning like the Sahara.

Inserting a smile in your lips,
you will look
and see a fine toreador!
And suddenly I,
from a bull's dying eye,
will fling my jealousy into the boxes.

If you carry your faltering steps to a bridge,
thinking
how good to be down there—
then it is I,
the Seine pouring under the bridge,
who call you,
baring my rotted teeth.

If you, driving fast with a man, burn up
the Strelka or the Sokolniki—⁵
then it is I, climbing high,
expectant and stripped like the moon, who make you
    yearn.

They will need
a strong man like me—
they will command:
get killed in the war!
The last word I shall speak
is your name,
blood clotted on my shrapnel-torn lip.

Shall my end be a crown?
Or Saint Helena?

Буре жизни оседлав валы,
я — равный кандидат
и на царя вселенной
и на
кандалы.

Быть царем назначено мне —
твое личико
на солнечном золоте моих монет
велю народу:
вычекань!
А там,
где тундрой мир вылинял,
где с северным ветром ведет река торги, —
на цепь нацарапаю имя Лилино
и цепь исцелую во мраке каторги.

Слушайте ж, забывшие, что небо голубо,
выщетинившиеся,
звери точно!
Это, может быть,
последняя в мире любовь
вызарилась румянцем чахоточного.

3

Забуду год, день, число.
Запрусь одинокий с листом бумаги я,
Творись, просветленных страданием слов
нечеловечья магия!

Сегодня, только вошел к вам,
почувствовал —

Having saddled the rollers of life's storm,
I'm now in the running
for the kingdom of the world
and
a convict's fetters.

I am fated to be a tsar—
on the sunlit gold of my coins
I shall command my subjects
to mint
your precious face!
But where
the earth fades into tundra,
where the river bargains with the North wind,
there I'll scratch Lily's name on my fetters,[6]
and in the darkness of hard labor, kiss them again
        and again.

Listen you, who have forgotten the sky is blue,
who have grown as hairy
as beasts.
This is, perhaps,
the very last love in the world
to dawn like a consumptive's flush.

3

I shall forget the year, the day, the date.
I shall lock myself up with a sheaf of paper.
Through the suffering of enlightened words,
do your creation, O inhuman magic!

This day, on visiting you,
I sensed

в доме неладно.
Ты что-то таила в шелковом платье,
и ширился в воздухе запах ладана.
Рада?
Холодное
«очень».
Смятеньем разбита разума ограда.
Я отчаянье громозжу, горящ и лихорадочен.

Послушай,
все равно
не спрячешь трупа.
Страшное слово на голову лавь!
Все равно
твой каждый мускул
как в рупор
трубит:
умерла, умерла, умерла!
Нет,
ответь.
Не лги!
(Как я такой уйду назад?)
Ямами двух могил
вырылись в лице твоем глаза.

Могилы глубятся.
Нету дна там.
Кажется,
рухну с пóмоста дней.
Я душу над пропастью натянул канатом,
жонглируя словами, закачался над ней.

Знаю,
любовь его износила уже.

something wrong in the house.
You had concealed something in your silks,
and the smell of incense expanded in the air.
Glad to see me?
That "very"
was very cool.
Confusion broke the barrier of reason.
Burning and feverish, I heaped on despair.

Listen,
whatever you do,
you cannot hide a corpse.
That terrible word pours lava on the head.
Whatever you do,
each sinew of yours
bugles
as from a megaphone:
she's dead, dead, dead!
It can't be,
answer me.
Don't lie!
(How can I go now?)
On your face your eyes excavate
the gaping hollows of two deep graves.

The graves grow deeper.
They have no bottom.
It seems
I shall plunge head first from the scaffolding of days.
Over the abyss I've stretched my soul in a tightrope
and, juggling with words, totter above it.

I know
love has already worn him out.

Скуку угадываю по стольким признакам.
Вымолоди себя в моей душе.
Празднику тела сердце вызнакомь.

Знаю,
каждый за женщину платит.
Ничего,
если пока
тебя вместо шика парижских платьев
одену в дым табака.

Любовь мою,
как апостол во время оно,
по тысяче тысяч разнесу дорог.
Тебе в веках уготована корона,
а в короне слова мои —
радугой судорог.

Как слоны стопудовыми играми
завершали победу Пиррову,
я поступью гения мозг твой выгромил.
Напрасно.
Тебя не вырву.

Радуйся,
радуйся,
ты доконала!
Теперь
такая тоска,
что только б добежать до канала
и голову сунуть воде в оскал.

Губы дала.
Как ты груба ими.
Прикоснулся и остыл.

I detect many signs of boredom.
Find your youth in my soul.
Invite the heart to the body's festival.

I know
each of us must pay for a woman.
Do you mind
if, in the meantime,
I clothe you in tobacco smoke
instead of Parisian chic.

My love,
like an apostle of olden days,
I'll carry down a thousand thousand roads.
Eternity for you has fashioned a crown,
and in that crown my words
spell a rainbow of shudders.

As elephants with hundredweight games
completed Pyrrhus' victory,
I sacked your brain with the tread of genius.
But in vain.
I cannot tear you out.

Rejoice,
rejoice,
now
you have finished me off!
My anguish is so sharp,
I'll run to the canal
and thrust my head in its maw.

You gave your lips.
You were so coarse with them.
I froze at the touch.

Будто целую покаянными губами
в холодных скалах высеченный монастырь.

Захлопали
двери.
Вошел он,
весельем улиц орошен.
Я
как надвое раскололся в вопле.
Крикнул ему:
«Хорошо!
Уйду!
Хорошо!
Твоя останется.
Тряпок нашей ей,
робкие крылья в шелках зажирели б.
Смотри, не уплыла б.
Камнем на шее
навесь жене жемчуга ожерелий!»

Ох, эта
ночь!
Отчаянье стягивал туже и туже сам.
От плача моего и хохота
морда комнаты выкосилась ужасом.

И видением вставал унесенный от тебя лик,
глазами вызарила ты на ковре его,
будто вымечтал какой-то новый Бялик
ослепительную царицу Сиона евреева.

В муке
перед той, которую отда́л,
коленопреклоненный выник.
Король Альберт,

With repentant lips I might have kissed
a monastery hacked from frigid rock.

Doors
banged.
He entered,
sprayed by the streets' gaiety.
I
split in a wail.
Cried out to him:
"All right,
I'll go,
all right!
Yours she'll remain.
Dress her up in fine rags,
and let shy wings, in silks, grow fat.
Watch out lest she float away.
Round your wife's neck,
like a stone, hang a necklace of pearls!"

Oh, what
a night!
I myself tightened the noose of despair.
My weeping and laughter
wrenched the room's face in horror.

The vision of your bereft countenance rose;
your eyes made it shine on the carpet
as if some new Byalik had conjured [7]
a dazzling Queen of Hebrew Zion.

In anguish
before her whom I had surrendered,
I went down on my knees.
King Albert,[8]

все города
отдавший,
рядом со мной задаренный именинник.

Вызолачивайтесь в солнце, цветы и травы!
Весеньтесь, жизни всех стихий!
Я хочу одной отравы —
пить и пить стихи.

Сердце обокравшая,
всего его лишив,
вымучившая душу в бреду мою,
прими мой дар, дорогая,
больше я, может быть, ничего не придумаю.

В праздник красьте сегодняшнее число.
Творись,
распятью равная магия.
Видите —
гвоздями слов
прибит к бумаге я.
(1915)

having surrendered
his cities,
is a gift-laden birthday boy compared with me.

Flowers and grasses, turn gold in the sun!
Be vernal, lives of all the elements!
I desire only one poison—
to drink the deep draught of verse.

Thief of my heart,
who have stripped it of everything,
who have tortured my soul in delirium,
accept, my dearest, this gift—
never, perhaps, shall I think of anything else.

Paint this day a bright holiday.
O crucifixionlike magic,
do your creation.
As you see—
the nails of words
nail me to paper.
(1915)

СЕБЕ, ЛЮБИМОМУ,
ПОСВЯЩАЕТ ЭТИ СТРОКИ АВТОР

Четыре.
Тяжелые, как удар.
«Кесарево кесарю — богу богово».
А такому,
как я,
ткнуться куда?
Где для меня уготовано логово?

Если б был я
маленький,
как Великий океан, —
на цыпочки б волн встал,
приливом ласкался к луне бы.
Где любимую найти мне,
такую, как и я?
Такая не уместилась бы в крохотное небо!

О, если б я нищ был!
Как миллиардер!
Что деньги душе?
Ненасытный вор в ней.
Моих желаний разнузданной орде
не хватит золота всех Калифорний.

Если б быть мне косноязычным,
как Дант
или Петрарка!
Душу к одной зажечь!
Стихами велеть истлеть ей!
И слова
и любовь моя —

TO HIS BELOVED SELF, THE AUTHOR DEDICATES THESE LINES[1]

Four words,
heavy as a blow:
". . . unto Caesar . . . unto god . . ."
But where can a man
like me
bury his head?
Where is there shelter for me?

If I were
as small
as the Great Ocean,
I'd tiptoe on the waves
and woo the moon like the tide.
Where shall I find a beloved,
a beloved like me?
She would be too big for the tiny sky!

Oh, to be poor!
Like a multimillionaire!
What's money to the soul?
In it dwells an insatiable thief.
The gold of all the Californias
will never satisfy the rapacious horde of my lusts.

Oh, to be tongued-tied
like Dante
or Petrarch!
I'd kindle my soul for one love alone!
In verse I'd command her to burn to ash!
And if my words
and my love

триумфальная арка:
пышно,
бесследно пройдут сквозь нее
любовницы всех столетий.

О, если б был я
тихий,
как гром, —
ныл бы,
дрожью объял бы земли одряхлевший скит.
Я
если всей его мощью
выреву голос огромный —
кометы заломят горящие руки,
бросятся вниз с тоски.

Я бы глаз лучами грыз ночи —
о, если б был я
тусклый,
как солнце!
Очень мне надо
сияньем моим поить
земли отощавшее лонце!

Пройду,
любовищу мою волоча.
В какой ночи́,
бредово́й,
недужной,
какими Голиафами я зача́т —
такой большой
и такой ненужный?
(1916)

were a triumphal arch,
then grandly
all the heroines of love through the ages
would pass through it, leaving no trace.

Oh, were I
as quiet
as thunder
then I would whine
and fold earth's aged hermitage in my shuddering
    embrace.
If,
to its full power,
I used my vast voice,
the comets would wring their burning hands
and plunge headlong in anguish.

With my eyes' rays I'd gnaw the night—
if I were, oh,
as dull
as the sun!
Why should I want
to feed with my radiance
the earth's lean lap!

I shall go by,
dragging my burden of love.
In what delirious
and ailing
night,
was I sired by Goliaths—
I, so large,
so unwanted?
(1916)

НЕОБЫЧАЙНОЕ ПРИКЛЮЧЕНИЕ, БЫВШЕЕ С ВЛАДИМИРОМ МАЯКОВСКИМ ЛЕТОМ НА ДАЧЕ

(Пушкино, Акулова гора, дача Румянцева,
27 верст по Ярославской жел. дор.)

В сто сорок солнц закат пылал,
в июль катилось лето,
была жара,
жара плыла —
на даче было это.
Пригорок Пушкино горбил
Акуловой горою,
а низ горы —
деревней был,
кривился крыш корою.
А за деревнею —
дыра,
и в ту дыру, наверно,
спускалось солнце каждый раз,
медленно и верно.
А завтра
снова
мир залить
вставало солнце а́ло.
И день за днем
ужасно злить
меня
вот это
стало.
И так однажды разозлясь,
что в страхе все поблекло,

AN EXTRAORDINARY ADVENTURE WHICH BEFELL VLADIMIR MAYAKOVSKY IN A SUMMER COTTAGE[1]

*(Pushkino, Akula's Mount, Rumyantsev Cottage,
27 versts on the Yaroslav Railway.)*

A hundred and forty suns in one sunset blazed,
and summer rolled into July;
it was so hot,
the heat swam in a haze—
and this was in the country.
Pushkino, a hillock, had for hump,
Akula, a large hill,
and at the hill's foot
a village stood—
crooked with the crust of roofs.
Beyond the village
gaped a hole
and into that hole, most likely,
the sun sank down each time,
faithfully and slowly.
And next morning,
to flood the world
anew,
the sun would rise all scarlet.
Day after day
this very thing
began
to rouse in me
great anger.
And flying into such a rage one day
that all things paled with fear,

в упор я крикнул солнцу:
«Слазь!
довольно шляться в пекло!»
Я крикнул солнцу:
«Дармоед!
занежен в облака ты,
а тут — не знай ни зим, ни лет,
сиди, рисуй плакаты!»
Я крикнул солнцу:
«Погоди!
послушай, златолобо,
чем так,
без дела заходить,
ко мне
на чай зашло бы!»
Что я наделал!
Я погиб!
Ко мне,
по доброй воле,
само,
раскинув луч-шаги,
шагает солнце в поле.
Хочу испуг не показать —
и ретируюсь задом.
Уже в саду его глаза.
Уже проходит садом.
В окошки,
в двери,
в щель войдя,
валилась солнца масса,
ввалилось;
дух переведя,
заговорило басом:
«Гоню обратно я огни
впервые с сотворенья.

I yelled at the sun point-blank:
"Get down!
Stop crawling into that hellhole!"
At the sun I yelled:
"You shiftless lump!
You're caressed by the clouds,
while here—winter and summer—
I must sit and draw these posters!"
I yelled at the sun again:
"Wait now!
Listen, goldbrow,
instead
of going down,
why not come down to tea
with me!"
What have I done!
I'm finished!
Toward me,
of his own good will,
himself,
spreading his beaming steps,
the sun strode across the field.
I tried to hide my fear,
and beat it backwards.
His eyes were in the garden now.
Then he passed through the garden.
His sun's mass pressing
through the windows,
doors,
and crannies,
in he rolled;
drawing a breath,
he spoke deep bass:
"For the first time since creation,
I drive the fires back.

Ты звал меня?
Чай гони,
гони, поэт, варенье!»
Слеза из глаз у самого —
жара с ума сводила,
но я ему —
на самовар:
«Ну что ж,
садись, светило!»
Черт дернул дерзости мои
орать ему, —
сконфужен,
я сел на уголок скамьи,
боюсь — не вышло б хуже!
Но странная из солнца ясь
струилась, —
и степенность
забыв,
сижу, разговорясь
с светилом постепенно.
Про то,
про это говорю,
что-де заела Роста,
а солнце:
«Ладно,
не горюй,
смотри на вещи просто!
А мне, ты думаешь,
светить
легко?
— Поди, попробуй! —
А вот идешь —
взялось идти,
идешь — и светишь в оба!»
Болтали так до темноты —

You called me?
Give me tea, poet,
spread out, spread out the jam!"
Tears gathered in my eyes—
the heat was maddening,
but pointing to the samovar,
I said to him:
"Well, sit down then,
luminary!"
The devil had prompted my insolence
to shout at him,
confused—
I sat on the edge of a bench;
I was afraid of worse!
But, from the sun, a strange radiance
streamed,
and forgetting
all formalities,
I sat chatting
with the luminary more freely.
Of this
and that I talked,
and of how I was swallowed up by Rosta,[2]
but the sun, he says:
"All right,
don't worry,
look at things more simply!
And do you think
I find it easy
to shine?
Just try it, if you will!—
You move along,
since move you must;
you move—and shine your eyes out!"
We gossiped thus till dark—

до бывшей ночи то есть.
Какая тьма уж тут?
На «ты»
мы с ним, совсем освоясь.
И скоро,
дружбы не тая,
бью по плечу его я.
А солнце тоже:
«Ты да я,
нас, товарищ, двое!
Пойдем, поэт,
взорим,
вспоем
у мира в сером хламе.
Я буду солнце лить свое,
а ты — свое,
стихами».
Стена теней,
ночей тюрьма
под солнц двустволкой пала.
Стихов и света кутерьма —
сияй во что попало!
Устанет то,
и хочет ночь
прилечь,
тупая сонница.
Вдруг — я
во всю светаю мочь —
и снова день трезвонится.
Светить всегда,
светить везде,
до дней последних донца,
светить —
и никаких гвоздей!
Вот лозунг мой —
и солнца!
(1920)

till former night, I mean.
For what darkness was there here?
We warmed up
to each other
and very soon,
openly displaying friendship,
I slapped him on the back.
The sun responded!
"You and I,
my comrade, are quite a pair!
Let's go, my poet,
let's dawn
and sing
in a gray tattered world.
I shall pour forth my sun,
and you—your own,
in verse."
A wall of shadows,
a jail of nights
fell under the double-barreled suns.
A commotion of verse and light—
shine all your worth!
Drowsy and dull,
one tired,
wanting to stretch out
for the night.
Suddenly—I
shone in all my might,
and morning rang its round.
Always to shine,
to shine everywhere,
to the very deeps of the last days,
to shine—
and to hell with everything else!
That is my motto—
and the sun's!
(1920)

ПРИКАЗ № 2 АРМИИ ИСКУССТВ

Это вам —
упитанные баритоны —
от Адама
до наших лет,
потрясающие театрами именуемые притоны
ариями Ромеов и Джульетт.

Это вам —
пентры,
раздобревшие как кони,
жрущая и ржущая России краса,
прячущаяся мастерскими,
по-старому драконя
цветочки и телеса.

Это вам —
прикрывшиеся листиками мистики,
лбы морщинками изрыв —
футуристики,
имажинистики,
акмеистики,
запутавшиеся в паутине рифм.
Это вам —
на растрепанные сменившим
гладкие прически,
на лапти — лак,
пролеткультцы,
кладущие заплатки
на вылинявший пушкинский фрак.

Это вам —
пляшущие, в дуду дующие,

144

ORDER NO. 2 TO THE ARMY OF THE ARTS[1]

This is for you—
the fleshy baritones
who, since the days
of Adam,
have shaken those dens called theaters
with the arias of Romeos and Juliets.

This is for you—
the *peintres,*
grown as robust as horses,
the ravening and neighing beauty of Russia,
skulking in ateliers
and, as of old, imposing Draconian laws on flowers
and bulking bodies.

This is for you—
who put on little fig leaves of mysticism,
whose brows are harrowed with wrinkles—
you, little futurists,
imaginists,
acmeists,[2]
entangled in the cobweb of rhymes.
This is for you—
who have exchanged rumpled hair
for a slick hairdo,
bast shoes for lacquered pumps,
you, men of the Proletcult,[3]
who keep patching
Pushkin's faded tailcoat.

This is for you—
who dance and pipe on pipes,

и открыто предающиеся,
и грешащие тайком,
рисующие себе грядущее
огромным академическим пайком.
Вам говорю
я —
гениален я или не гениален,
бросивший безделушки
и работающий в Росте,
говорю вам —
пока вас прикладами не прогнали:
Бросьте!

Бросьте!
Забудьте,
плюньте
и на рифмы,
и на арии,
и на розовый куст,
и на прочие мелехлюндии
из арсеналов искусств.
Кому это интересно,
что — «Ах, вот бедненький!
Как он любил
и каким он был несчастным...»?
Мастера,
а не длинноволосые проповедники
нужны сейчас нам.
Слушайте!
Паровозы стонут,
дует в щели и в пол:
«Дайте уголь с Дону!
Слесарей,
механиков в депо!»

sell yourselves openly,
sin in secret,
and picture your future as academicians
with outsized rations.
I admonish you,
I—
genius or not—
who have forsaken trifles
and work in Rosta,[4]
I admonish you—
before they disperse you with rifle-butts:
Give it up!

Give it up!
Forget it.
Spit
on rhymes
and arias
and the rose bush
and other such mawkishness
from the arsenal of the arts.
Who's interested now
in—"Ah, wretched soul!
How he loved,
how he suffered . . ."?
Good workers—
these are the men we need
rather than long-haired preachers.
Listen!
The locomotives groan,
and a draft blows through crannies and floor:
"Give us coal from the Don!
Metal workers
and mechanics for the depot!"

У каждой реки на истоке,
лежа с дырой в боку,
пароходы провыли доки:
«Дайте нефть из Баку!»
Пока канителим, спорим,
смысл сокровенный ища:
«Дайте нам новые формы!» —
несется вопль по вещам.

Нет дураков,
ждя, что выйдет из уст его,
стоять перед «маэстрами» толпой разинь.
Товарищи,
дайте новое искусство —
такое,
чтобы выволочь республику из грязи.
(1921)

At each river's outlet, steamers
with an aching hole in their side,
howl through the docks:
"Give us oil from Baku!"
While we dawdle and quarrel
in search of fundamental answers,
all things yell:
"give us new forms!"

There are no fools today
to crowd, open-mouthed, round a "maestro"
and await his pronouncement.
Comrades,
give us a new form of art—
an art
that will pull the republic out of the mud.
(1921)

ЛЮБЛЮ

ОБЫКНОВЕННО ТАК

Любовь любому рожденному дадена, —
но между служб,
доходов
и прочего
со дня на́ день
очерствевает сердечная почва.
На сердце тело надето,
на тело — рубаха.
Но и этого мало!
Один —
идиот! —
манжеты наделал
и груди стал заливать крахмалом.
Под старость спохватятся.
Женщина мажется.
Мужчина по Мюллеру мельницей машется.
Но поздно.
Морщинами множится кожица.
Любовь поцветет,
поцветет —
и скукожится.

МАЛЬЧИШКОЙ

Я в меру любовью был одаренный.
Но с детства
людьё
трудами муштровано.
А я —
убёг на берег Риона

I LOVE[1]

USUALLY SO

Any man born is entitled to love,
but what with jobs,
incomes,
and other such things,
the heart's core grows harder
from day to day.
The heart wears a body;
the body—a shirt.
Even that's not enough!
Someone—
the idiot!—
manufactured stiff cuffs
and clamped starch on the chest.
Aging, people suddenly have second thoughts.
Women rub in powder and rouge.
Men do cartwheels according to Müller's system.[2]
But it's too late.
The skin proliferates in wrinkles.
Love flowers,
and flowers
and then withers and shrinks.

AS A BOY

I was gifted in measure with love.
Since childhood,
people
have been drilled to labor.
But I
fled to the banks of the Rion[3]

и шлялся,
ни чёрта не делая ровно.
Сердилась мама:
«Мальчишка паршивый!»
Грозился папаша поясом выстегать.
А я,
разживясь трехрублевкой фальшивой,
играл с солдатьём под забором в «три листика».
Без груза рубах,
без машмачного груза
жарился в кутаисском зное.
Вворачивал солнцу то спину,
то пузо —
пока под ложечкой не заноет.
Дивилось солнце:
«Чуть виден весь-то!
А тоже —
с сердечком.
Старается малым!
Откуда
в этом
в аршине
место —
и мне,
и реке,
и стовёрстым скалам?!»

ЮНОШЕЙ

Юношеству занятий масса.
Грамматикам учим дурней и дур мы.
Меня ж
из 5-го вышибли класса.
Пошли швырять в московские тюрьмы.

and knocked about there,
doing absolutely nothing.
Mamma chided me angrily:
"Good for nothing!"
Papa threatened to belt me.
But I,
laying my hands on a false three-ruble note,
played at "three leaves" with soldiers under a fence.[4]
Unconstricted by shirt,
unburdened by boots,
I was baked by the sultry sun of Kutaisi.[5]
To the sun I proffered now my back,
now my belly,
until the pit of my stomach ached.
The sun was astonished:
"I can hardly see him, the brat!
Yet he's got
a little heart too.
He does his small best!
Where,
in less
than a yard
is there place
for me
and the river
and the hundred-mile stretch of rock?!"

AS A YOUNG MAN

Youth has a mass of occupations.
We hammer grammar into the thickest skulls.
But I
was expelled from the fifth class.
Then they began to shove me into Moscow prisons.

В вашем
квартирном
маленьком мирике
для спален растут кучерявые лирики.
Что выищешь в этих болоночьих лириках?!
Меня вот
любить
учили
в Бутырках.
Что мне тоска о Булонском лесе?!
Что мне вздох от видов на́ море?!
Я вот
в «Бюро похоронных процессий»
влюбился
в глазок 103 камеры.
Глядят ежедневное солнце,
зазна́ются.
«Чего — мол — стоят лучёнышки эти?»
А я
за стенного
за желтого зайца
отдал тогда бы — все на свете.

МОЙ УНИВЕРСИТЕТ

Французский знаете.
Де́лите.
Множите.
Склоняете чу́дно.
Ну и склоняйте!
Скажите —
а с домом спеться
можете?
Язык трамвайский вы понимаете?

In your
cosy
little apartment world,
curly-headed lyricists sprout in bedrooms.
What do you find in these lapdog lyricists?!
As for me,
I learned
about love
in Butyrki.[6]
Does nostalgia for the Bois de Boulogne mean any-
    thing?!
Or to gaze at the sea and sigh?!
In the "Funeral Parlor," [7]
I
fell in love
with the keyhole of Cell 103.[8]
Staring at the daily sun,
people ask:
"How much do they cost, these little sunbeams?"
But I
for a yellow patch
of light jumping on the wall
would then have given everything in the world.

MY UNIVERSITY

French you know.
You divide.
Multiply.
You decline wonderfully.
Well, decline then!
But tell me—
can you sing in tune
with a house?
Do you understand the idiom of tramcars?

Птенец человечий,
чуть только вывелся —
за книжки рукой,
за тетрадные дести.
А я обучался азбуке с вывесок,
листая страницы железа и жести.
Землю возьмут,
обкорнав,
ободрав ее —
учат.
И вся она — с крохотный глобус.
А я
боками учил географию —
недаром же
наземь
ночёвкой хлопаюсь!
Мутят Иловайских больные вопросы:
— Была ль рыжа борода Барбароссы? —
Пускай!
Не копаюсь в пропыленном вздоре я —
любая в Москве мне известна история!
Берут Добролюбова (чтоб зло ненавидеть), —
фамилья ж против,
скулит родовая.
Я
жирных
с детства привык ненавидеть,
всегда себя
за обед продавая.
Научатся,
сядут —
чтоб нравиться даме,
мыслишки звякают лбёнками медненькими.
А я
говорил

The human fledgling—
barely out of the egg—
grasps at a book,
at quires of exercise paper.
But I learned my alphabet from signboards,
leafing through pages of iron and tin.
People take the earth,
trim
and strip it—
and they teach you a lesson.
It's just a tiny globe.
But I
learned my geography with my ribs—
no wonder I
flop down to earth
for my night's rest!
Painful questions torment the Ilovaiskys:[9]
Did Barbarossa have a red beard?—
What if he did!
I do not rummage in dust-laden rubbish—
I know all the histories in Moscow!
They take Dobrolyubov (to hate evil),[10]
but the name objects,
the family whimpers.
Since childhood,
I've always hated
the overfed,
for I always had to sell myself
for a meal.
They learn
to sit down—
to please a lady;
their trifling thoughts clink against tinpot foreheads.
But I
talked

с одними домами.
Одни водокачки мне собеседниками.
Окном слуховым внимательно слушая,
ловили крыши — что брошу в уши я.
А после
о ночи
и друг о друге
трещали,
язык ворочая — флюгер.

ВЗРОСЛОЕ

У взрослых дела.
В рублях карманы.
Любить?
Пожалуйста!
Рубликов за́ сто.
А я,
бездомный,
ручища
в рваный
в карман засунул
и шлялся, глазастый.
Ночь.
Надеваете лучшее платье.
Душой отдыхаете на женах, на вдовах.
Меня
Москва душила в объятьях
кольцом своих бесконечных Садовых.
В сердца,
в часишки
любовницы тикают.
В восторге партнеры любовного ложа.
Столиц сердцебиение дикое
ловил я,

only to houses.
Water towers were my only company.
Listening closely with their dormer windows,
the roofs caught what I threw in their ears.
Afterwards,
they prattled
about the night
and about each other,
wagging their weathercock tongue.

ADULTS

Adults have much to do.
Their pockets are stuffed with rubles.
Love?
Certainly!
For about a hundred rubles.
But I,
homeless,
thrust
my hands
into my torn pockets
and slouched about, goggle-eyed.
Night.
You put on your best dress.
You relax with wives and widows.
Moscow,
with the ring of its endless Sadovayas,[11]
choked me in its embraces.
The hearts
of amorous women
go tic-toc.
On a bed of love the partners feel ecstatic.
Stretched out like Passion Square,[12]
I caught the wild heartbeat of capital cities.

Страстною площадью лёжа.
Враспашку —
сердце почти что снаружи —
себя открываю и солнцу и луже.
Входите страстями!
Любовями влазьте!
Отныне я сердцем править не властен.
У прочих знаю сердца дом я.
Оно в груди — любому известно!
На мне ж
с ума сошла анатомия.
Сплошное сердце —
гудит повсеместно.
О, сколько их,
одних только вёсен,
за 20 лет в распалённого ввалено!
Их груз нерастраченный — просто несносен.
Несносен не так,
для стиха,
а буквально.

ЧТО ВЫШЛО

Больше чем можно,
больше чем надо —
будто
поэтовым бредом во сне навис —
комок сердечный разросся громадой:
громада любовь,
громада ненависть.
Под ношей
ноги
шагали шатко —

Open wide—
my heart nearly on the surface—
I unfolded myself to sun and puddle.
Enter me with your passions!
Climb in with your loves!
Now I have lost control of my heart.
I know where lodges the heart in others.
In the breast—as everyone knows!
But with me
anatomy has gone mad:
nothing but heart
roaring everywhere.
Oh, what a multitude
of springtimes
has been packed into my feverish body in these 20
    years!
Their burden unspent is simply unbearable.
Unbearable not figuratively,
in verse,
but literally.

WHAT HAPPENED

More than possible,
more than necessary—
as though
in sleep sagging down in poetic delirium—
the lump of the heart has grown huge in bulk:
that bulk is love,
that bulk is hate.
Under the burden
my legs
walked shakily—

ты знаешь,
я же
ладно слажен —
и всё же
тащусь сердечным придатком,
плеч подгибая косую сажень.
Взбухаю стихов молоком
— и не вылиться —
некуда, кажется — полнится заново.
Я вытомлен лирикой —
мира кормилица,
гипербола
праобраза Мопассанова.

ЗОВУ

Поднял силачом,
понес акробатом.
Как избирателей сзывают на митинг,
как сёла
в пожар
созывают набатом —
я звал:
«А вот оно!
Вот!
Возьмите!»
Когда
такая махина ахала —
не глядя,
пылью,
грязью,
сугробом
дамьё
от меня
ракетой шарахалось:
«Нам чтобы поменьше,

as you know,
I am
well built—
and yet,
an appendage of the heart, I dragged myself about,
hunching the vast width of my shoulders.
I swell with the milk of verse—
there's no pouring it forth—
anywhere, it seems—and it brims me anew.
I am exhausted by lyricism—
wet nurse of the world,
the hyperbole
of Maupassant's archetype.[13]

I CALL

I raised it like a strong man,
carried it like an acrobat.
As electors are called to a meeting,
as the tocsin
summons village folk
to a fire—
so I called out:
"Here it is!
Here!
Take it!"
Whenever
this clumsy bulk groaned—
without looking,
through dust,
through dirt,
through snowdrift,
the ladies
shied away from me
like a rocket:
"We'd prefer something smaller;

нам вроде танго́ бы...»
Нести не могу —
и несу мою ношу.
Хочу ее бросить —
и знаю,
не брошу!
Распора не сдержат рёбровы дуги.
Грудная клетка трещала с натуги.

ТЫ

Пришла —
деловито,
за рыком,
за ростом,
взглянув,
разглядела просто мальчика.
Взяла,
отобрала сердце
и просто
пошла играть —
как девочка мячиком.
И каждая —
чудо будто видится —
где дама вкопалась,
а где девица.
«Такого любить?
Да этакий ринется!
Должно, укротительница.
Должно, из зверинца!»
А я ликую.
Нет его —
ига!
От радости себя не помня,

we'd rather have a tango . . ."
I cannot bear the burden—
but I bear it.
I should like to throw it down—
but I know
I shall not throw it down!
My ribs' staves will not stand the thrust.
The cage of the chest cracks under the strain.

YOU

You came—
determined,
because I was large,
because I was roaring,
but on close inspection
you saw a mere boy.
You seized
and snatched away my heart
and began
to play with it—
like a girl with a bouncing ball.
And before this miracle
every woman
was either a lady astounded
or a maiden inquiring:
"Love such a fellow?
Why, he'll pounce on you!
She must be a lion tamer,
a girl from the zoo!"
But I was triumphant.
I didn't feel it—
the yoke!
Oblivious with joy,

скакал,
индейцем свадебным прыгал,
так было весело,
было легко мне.

НЕВОЗМОЖНО

Один не смогу —
не снесу рояля
(тем более —
несгораемый шкаф).
А если не шкаф,
не рояль,
то я ли
сердце снес бы, обратно взяв.
Банкиры знают:
«Богаты без края мы.
Карманов не хватит —
кладем в несгораемый».
Любовь
в тебя —
богатством в железо —
запрятал,
хожу
и радуюсь Крезом.
И разве,
если захочется очень,
улыбку возьму,
пол-улыбки
и мельче,
с другими кутя,
протрачу в полно́чи
рублей пятнадцать лирической мелочи.

I jumped
and leapt about, a bride-happy redskin,
I felt so elated
and light.

IMPOSSIBLE

I can't do it alone—
carry the grand piano
(and even less,
the safe).
But if I can't manage the safe
or the grand piano,
then, having retrieved it,
how can I carry my heart.
Bankers know:
"We're boundlessly rich.
If we don't have enough pockets,
we can stuff our safes."
In you—
I have hidden
my love,
like riches in steel,
and I walk about
exulting, a Croesus.
And,
if desire insist
I can draw out a smile,
a half-smile,
even less,
and, in company reveling,
in half a night expend
some fifteen rubles' worth of lyrical change.

ТАК И СО МНОЙ

Флоты — и то стекаются в гавани.
Поезд — и то к вокзалу гонит.
Ну, а меня к тебе и подавней
— я же люблю! —
тянет и клонит.
Скупой спускается пушкинский рыцарь
подвалом своим любоваться и рыться.
Так я
к тебе возвращаюсь, любимая.
Мое это сердце,
любуюсь моим я.
Домой возвращаетесь радостно.
Грязь вы
с себя соскребаете, бреясь и моясь.
Так я
к тебе возвращаюсь, —
разве,
к тебе идя,
не иду домой я?!
Земных принимает земное лоно.
К конечной мы возвращаемся цели.
Так я
к тебе
тянусь неуклонно,
еле расстались,
развиделись еле.

ВЫВОД

Не смоют любовь
ни ссоры,
ни вёрсты.
Продумана,

IT'S THAT WAY WITH ME

Fleets! They too flow to port.
A train likewise speeds to a station.
And I, even more, am pulled and tugged
towards you—
for I love.
Pushkin's covetous knight[14]
visits his cellar to rummage and gloat.
In the same way,
my beloved,
I return to you.
This is my heart,
and I marvel at it.
People gladly go home
and scrape off their dirt,
washing and shaving.
In the same way
I return to you—
for in going towards you,
am I not returning home?!
Man of earth in earth is laid.
We return to our destination.
Thus steadily
I am drawn back
towards you
as soon as we part
or stop seeing each other.

CONCLUSION

Neither quarrels,
nor miles,
can wash away love.
It has been deeply thought,

выверена,
проверена.
Подъемля торжественно стих строкопёстрый,
клянусь —
люблю
неизменно и верно!
(1922)

tested,
checked.
Solemnly raising index-lined verse,
I swear—
I love
immutably, truly!
(1922)

БРУКЛИНСКИЙ МОСТ

Издай, Кулидж,
радостный клич!
На хорошее
                и мне не жалко слов.
От похвал
        красней,
              как Флага нашего матёрийка,
хоть вы
       и разъюнайтед стетс
                  оф
Америка.
Как в церковь
         идет
           помешавшийся верующий,
как в скит
       удаляется,
            строг и прост, —
так я
     в вечерней
          сереющей мерещи
вхожу,
     смиренный, на Бруклинский мост.
Как в город
       в сломанный
            прет победитель
на пушках — жерлом
          жирафу под рост —
так, пьяный славой,
        так жить в аппетите,
влезаю,
    гордый,

172

BROOKLYN BRIDGE[1]

Give, Coolidge,
a shout of joy!
I too will spare no words
                    about good things.
Blush
        at my praise,
                    go red as our flag,
however
                    united-states
                                -of
-america you may be.
As a crazed believer
                    enters
                                a church,
retreats
        into a monastery cell,
                    austere and plain;
so I,
        in graying evening
                    haze,
humbly set foot
                    on Brooklyn Bridge.
As a conqueror presses
                    into a city
                                all shattered,
on cannon with muzzles
                    craning high as a giraffe—
so, drunk with glory,
                    eager to live,
I clamber,
            in pride,

на Бруклинский мост.
Как глупый художник
                    в мадонну музея
вонзает глаз свой,
                    влюблен и остр,
так я,
      с поднебесья,
                    в звезды усеян,
смотрю
        на Нью-Йорк
                    сквозь Бруклинский мост.
Нью-Йорк
        до вечера тяжек
                        и душен,
забыл,
      что тяжко ему
                    и высо́ко,
и только одни
            домовьи души
встают
      в прозрачном свечении о́кон.
Здесь
      еле зудит
                элевейтеров зуд.
И только
        по этому
                тихому зуду
поймешь —
            поезда́
                с дребезжаньем ползут,
как будто
        в буфет убирают посуду.
Когда ж,
        казалось, с под речки на́чатой
развозит

174

                         upon Brooklyn Bridge.
As a foolish painter
                    plunges his eye,
sharp and loving,
                    into a museum madonna,
so I,
      from the near skies
                         bestrewn with stars,
gaze
      at New York
                    through the Brooklyn Bridge.
New York,
          heavy and stifling
                              till night,
has forgotten
              its hardships
                             and height;
and only
         the household ghosts
ascend
       in the lucid glow of its windows.
Here
      the elevateds
                    drone softly.
And only
         their gentle
                       droning
tell us:
        here trains
                    are crawling and rattling
like dishes
            being cleared into a cupboard.
While
      a shopkeeper fetched sugar
from a mill

с фабрики
           сахар лавочник, —
то
   под мостом проходящие мачты
размером
           не больше размеров булавочных.
Я горд
      вот этой
              стальною милей,
живьем в ней
              мои видения встали —
борьба
      за конструкции
                    вместо стилей,
расчет суровый
              гаек
              и стали.
Если
    придет
          окончание света —
планету
      хаос
          разделает влоск,
и только
        один останется
                      этот
над пылью гибели вздыбленный мост,
то,
   как из косточек,
                  тоньше иголок,
тучнеют
       в музеях стоящие
                        ящеры,
так
   с этим мостом
                столетий геолог

        that seemed to project
                out of the water—
the masts
        passing under the bridge
looked
      no larger than pins.
I am proud
        of just this
             mile of steel;
upon it,
      my visions come to life, erect—
here's a fight
        for construction
            instead of style,
an austere disposition
        of bolts
          and steel.
If
  the end of the world
           befall—
and chaos
      smash our planet
            to bits,
and what remains
      will be
        this
bridge, rearing above the dust of destruction;
then,
    as huge ancient lizards
           are rebuilt
from bones
      finer than needles,
         to tower in museums,
so,
  from this bridge,
      a geologist of the centuries

сумел
    воссоздать бы
                  дни настоящие.
Он скажет:
        — Вот эта
             стальная лапа
соединяла
    моря и прерии,
отсюда
    Европа
        рвалась на Запад,
пустив
    по ветру
           индейские перья.
Напомнит
    машину
        ребро вот это —
сообразите,
        хватит рук ли,
чтоб, став,
        стальной ногой
             на Мангéтен,
к себе
    за губу
        притягивать Брýклин?
По проводам
        электрической пряди —
я знаю —
    эпоха
        после пара —
здесь
    люди
        уже
           орали по радио,

will succeed
                in recreating
                                our contemporary world.
He will say:
                —Yonder paw
                                of steel
once joined
                the seas and the prairies;
from this spot,
                Europe
                        rushed to the West,
scattering
            to the wind
                        Indian feathers.
This rib
        reminds us
                    of a machine—
just imagine,
                would there be hands enough,
after planting
                a steel foot
                            in Manhattan,
to yank
        Brooklyn to oneself
                            by the lip?
By the cables
                of electric strands,
I recognize
            the era succeeding
                            the steam age—
here
    men
        had ranted
                    on radio.

здесь
    люди
        уже
            взлетали по аэро.
Здесь
    жизнь
        была
            одним — беззаботная,
другим —
      голодный
            протяжный вой.
Отсюда
    безработные
в Гудзон
      кидались
          вниз головой.
И дальше
    картина моя
          без загвоздки
по струнам-канатам,
        аж звездам к ногам.
Я вижу —
    здесь
      стоял Маяковский,
стоял
    и стихи слагал по слогам. —
Смотрю,
    как в поезд глядит эскимос,
впиваюсь,
    как в ухо впивается клещ.
Бру́клинский мост —
да...
    Это вещь!
(1925)

Here
　　men
　　　　had ascended
　　　　　　　　in planes.
For some,
　　　　life
　　　　　　here
　　　　　　　　had no worries;
for others,
　　　　　it was a prolonged
　　　　　　　　　and hungry howl.
From this spot,
　　　　　　jobless men
leapt
　　headlong
　　　　into the Hudson.[2]
Now
　　my canvas
　　　　　is unobstructed
as it stretches on cables of string
　　　　　　　　　　to the feet of the stars.
I see:
　　here
　　　　stood Mayakovsky,
stood,
　　　composing verse, syllable by syllable.
I stare
　　　as an Eskimo gapes at a train,
I seize on it
　　　　　as a tick fastens to an ear.
Brooklyn Bridge—
yes . . .
　　　　That's quite a thing!
(1925)

ДОМОЙ!

Уходите, мысли, во-свояси.
Обнимись,
    души и моря глубь.
Тот,
  кто постоянно ясен —
тот,
  по-моему,
      просто глуп.
Я в худшей каюте
       из всех кают —
всю ночь надо мною
       ногами куют.
Всю ночь,
   покой потолка возмутив,
несется танец,
     стонет мотив:
«Маркита,
    Маркита,
Маркита моя,
зачем ты,
   Маркита,
не любишь меня...»
А зачем
   любить меня Марките?!
У меня
  и франков даже нет.
А Маркиту
   (толечко моргните!)
зá сто франков
      препроводят в кабинет.
Небольшие деньги —
     поживи для шику —

BACK HOME![1]

Thoughts, go your way home.
Embrace,
          depths of the soul and the sea.
In my view,
          it is
               stupid
to be
     always serene.
My cabin is the worst
                    of all cabins—
all night above me
                    thuds a smithy of feet.
All night,
          stirring the ceiling's calm,
dancers stampede
                    to a moaning motif:
"Marquita,
          Marquita,
Marquita, my darling,
why won't you,
          Marquita,
why won't you love me . . ."
But why
     should Marquita love me?!
I have
     no francs to spare.
And Marquita
               (at the slightest wink!)
for a hundred francs
                    she'd be brought to your room.
The sum's not large—
                    just live for show—

нет,
	интеллигент,
			взбивая грязь вихров,
будешь всучивать ей
				швейную машинку,
по стежкам
		строчащую
				шелка́ стихов.
Пролетарии
		приходят к коммунизму
					низом —
низом шахт,
		серпов
			и вил, —
я ж
	с небес поэзии
			бросаюсь в коммунизм,
потому что
		нет мне
			без него любви.
Все равно —
		сослался сам я
				или послан к маме —
слов ржавеет сталь,
			чернеет баса медь.
Почему
	под иностранными дождями
вымокать мне,
		гнить мне
				и ржаветь?
Вот лежу,
		уехавший за во́ды,
ленью

no,
    you highbrow,
                ruffling your matted hair,
you would thrust upon her
                  a sewing machine,
in stitches
        scribbling
             the silk of verse.
Proletarians
        arrive at communism
                from below—
by the low way of mines,
             sickles,
                and pitchforks—
but I,
       from poetry's skies,
              plunge into communism,
because
        without it
            I feel no love.
Whether
       I'm self-exiled
             or sent to mamma—
the steel of words corrodes,
            the brass of the bass tarnishes.
Why,
      beneath foreign rains,
must I soak,
        rot,
          and rust?
Here I recline,
          having gone oversea,
in my idleness

еле двигаю
моей машины части.
Я себя
советским чувствую
заводом,
вырабатывающим счастье.
Не хочу,
чтоб меня, как цветочек с полян,
рвали
после служебных тягот.
Я хочу,
чтоб в дебатах
потел Госплан,
мне давая
задания на́ год.
Я хочу,
чтоб над мыслью
времен комиссар
с приказанием нависал.
Я хочу,
чтоб сверхставками спе́ца
получало
любовищу сердце.
Я хочу,
чтоб в конце работы
завком
запирал мои губы
замком.
Я хочу,
чтоб к штыку
приравняли перо.
С чугуном чтоб
и с выделкой стали
о работе стихов,

        barely moving
                my machine parts.
I myself
      feel like a Soviet
             factory,
manufacturing happiness.
I object
      to being torn up,
like a flower of the fields,
             after a long day's work.
I want
      the Gosplan to sweat[2]
             in debate,
assigning me
        goals a year ahead.
I want
      a commissar
          with a decree
to lean over the thought of the age.
I want
      the heart to earn
its love wage
        at a specialist's rate.
I want
      the factory committee
             to lock
my lips
      when the work is done.
I want
      the pen to be on a par
             with the bayonet;
and Stalin
      to deliver his Politbureau
reports

от Политбюро,
чтобы делал
                доклады Сталин.
«Так, мол,
            и так...
                        И до самых верхов
прошли
        из рабочих нор мы:
в Союзе
        Республик
                    пониманье стихов
выше
        довоенной нормы...»
(1925)

      about verse in the making
as he would about pig iron
                      and the smelting of steel.
"That's how it is,
           the way it goes. . . .
                        We've attained
the topmost level,
           climbing from the workers' bunks:
in the Union
         of Republics
              the understanding of verse
now tops
      the prewar norm . . ." [3]
(1925)

РАЗГОВОР С ФИНИНСПЕКТОРОМ О ПОЭЗИИ

Гражданин фининспектор!
                    Простите за беспокойство.
Спасибо...
            не тревожьтесь...
                        я постою...
У меня к вам
            дело
                деликатного свойства:
о месте
        поэта
            в рабочем строю.
В ряду
        имеющих
                лабазы и угодья
и я обложен
            и должен караться.
Вы требуете
            с меня
                    пятьсот в полугодие
и двадцать пять
                за неподачу деклараций.
Труд мой
        любому
                труду
                        родствен.
Взгляните —
            сколько я потерял,
какие
        издержки
            в моем производстве

CONVERSATION WITH A TAX COLLECTOR ABOUT POETRY[1]

Citizen tax collector!
                    Forgive my bothering you . . .
Thank you . . .
                don't worry . . .
                            I'll stand . . .
My business
            is
                of a delicate nature:
about the place
                of the poet
                            in the workers' ranks.
Along with
            owners
                of stores and property
I'm made subject
                to taxes and penalties.
You demand
            I pay
                five hundred for the half year
and twenty-five
                for failing to send in my returns.
Now
    my work
            is like
                any other work.
Look here—
            how much I've lost,
what
    expenses
            I have in my production

и сколько тратится
                на материал.
Вам,
     конечно, известно
                     явление «рифмы».
Скажем,
        строчка
              окончилась словом
                            «отца»,
и тогда
       через строчку,
                    слога повторив, мы
ставим
       какое-нибудь:
                   ламцадрица-ца́.
Говоря по-вашему,
                 рифма —
                       вексель.
Учесть через строчку! —
                       вот распоряжение.
И ищешь
        мелочишку суффиксов и флексий
в пустующей кассе
                 склонений
                          и спряжений.
Начнешь это
           слово
               в строчку всовывать,
а оно не лезет —
               нажал и сломал.
Гражданин фининспектор,
                       честное слово,
поэту
     в копеечку влетают слова.

and how much I spend
                    on materials.
You know,
        of course,
                    about "rhyme."
Suppose
        a line
                ends with the word
                            "day,"
and then,
        repeating the syllables
                            in the third line,
we insert
        something like
                    "tarara-boom-de-ay."
In your idiom,
                rhyme
                    is a bill of exchange
to be honored in the third line!—
                            that's the rule.
And so you hunt
        for the small change of suffixes and flections
in the depleted cashbox
                    of conjugations
                            and declensions.
You start shoving
                a word
                        into the line,
but it's a tight fit—
                    you press and it breaks.
Citizen tax collector,
                    honestly,
the poet
        spends a fortune on words.

Говоря по-нашему,
                    рифма —
                            бочка.
Бочка с динамитом.
                    Строчка —
                            фитиль.
Строка додымит,
                взрывается строчка, —
и город
        на воздух
                строфой летит.
Где найдешь,
            на какой тариф,
рифмы,
        чтоб враз убивали, нацелясь?
Может,
        пяток
                небывалых рифм
только и остался
                что в Венецуэле.
И тянет
        меня
                в холода и в зной.
Бросаюсь,
            опутан в авансы и в займы я.
Гражданин,
            учтите билет проездной!
— Поэзия
            — вся —
                езда в незнаемое.
Поэзия —
            та же добыча радия.
В грамм добыча,
                в год труды.
Изводишь

194

In our idiom
                rhyme
                        is a keg.
A keg of dynamite.
                    The line
                            is a fuse.
The line burns to the end
                        and explodes,
and the town
            is blown sky-high
                            in a strophe.
Where can you find,
                and at what price,
rhymes
        that take aim and kill on the spot?
Suppose
        only a half dozen
                        unheard-of rhymes
were left
        in, say, Venezuela.
And so
        I'm drawn
                to North and South.
I rush around
            entangled in advances and loans.
Citizen!
        Consider my traveling expenses.
—Poetry—
            —all of it!—
                        is a journey to the unknown.
Poetry
    is like mining radium.
For every gram
                you work a year.
For the sake of a single word

единого слова ради
тысячи тонн
           словесной руды.
Но как
      испепеляюще
                слов этих жжение
рядом
      с тлением
                слова-сырца.
Эти слова
           приводят в движение
тысячи лет
           миллионов сердца.
Конечно,
           различны поэтов сорта.
У скольких поэтов
                легкость руки!
Тянет,
      как фокусник,
                    строчку изо рта
и у себя
      и у других.
Что говорить
           о лирических кастратах?!
Строчку
      чужую
           вставит — и рад.
Это
   обычное
           воровство и растрата
среди охвативших страну растрат.
Эти
   сегодня
           стихи и оды,
в аплодисментах
                ревомые ревмя,

you waste
a thousand tons
of verbal ore.
But how
incendiary
the burning of these words
compared
with the smoldering
of the raw material.
These words
will move
millions of hearts
for thousands of years.
Of course,
there are many kinds of poets.
So many of them
use legerdemain!
And,
like conjurers,
pull lines from their mouths—
their own—
and other people's.
Not to speak
of the lyrical castrates?!
They're only too glad
to shove in
a borrowed line.
This is
just one more case
of robbery and embezzlement
among the frauds rampant in the country.
These
verses and odes
bawled out
today
amidst applause,

войдут
        в историю
                    как накладные расходы
на сделанное
                нами —
                        двумя или тремя.
Пуд,
    как говорится,
                    соли столовой
съешь
    и сотней папирос клуби,
чтобы
        добыть
                драгоценное слово
из артезианских
                людских глубин.
И сразу
        ниже
            налога рост.
Скиньте
        с обложенья
                    нуля колесо!
Рубль девяносто
                сотня папирос,
рубль шестьдесят
                    столовая соль.
В вашей анкете
                вопросов масса:
— Были выезды?
                    Или выездов нет? —
А что,
    если я
            десяток пегасов
загнал

                    will go down
in history
              as the overhead expenses
of what
          two or three of us
                        have achieved.
As the saying goes,
                  you eat forty pounds
                              of table salt,[2]
and smoke
          a hundred cigarettes
in order
        to dredge up
                    one precious word
from artesian
            human depths.
So at once
          my tax
                  shrinks.
Strike out
          one wheeling zero
                            from the balance due!
For a hundred cigarettes—
                        a ruble ninety;
for table salt—
              a ruble sixty.
Your form
          has a mass of questions:
"Have you traveled on business
                          or not?"
But suppose
          I have
                  ridden to death
a hundred Pegasi

за последние
15 лет?
У вас —
в мое положение войдите —
про слуг
и имущество
с этого угла.
А что,
если я
народа водитель
и одновреме́нно —
народный слуга?
Класс
гласит
из слова из нашего,
а мы,
пролетарии,
двигатели пера.
Машину
души
с годами изнашиваешь.
Говорят:
— в архив,
исписался,
пора! —
Все меньше любится,
все меньше дерзается,
и лоб мой
время
с разбега круши́т.
Приходит
страшнейшая из амортизаций —
амортизация
сердца и души.
И когда

                    in the last
                              15 years?
And here you have—
                    imagine my feelings!—
something
          about servants
                         and assets.
But what if I am
                 simultaneously
                               a leader
and a servant
              of the people?
The working class
                  speaks
                         through my mouth,
and we,
         proletarians,
                       are drivers of the pen.
As the years go by,
                    you wear out
                                 the machine of the soul.
And people say:
                "A back number,
                                 he's written out,
                                 he's through!"
There's less and less love,
                            and less and less daring,
and time
         is a battering ram
                            against my head.
Then there's amortization,
                           the deadliest of all;
amortization
             of the heart and soul.
And when

это солнце
                разжиревшим боровом
взойдет
        над грядущим
                        без нищих и калек, —
я
  уже
      сгнию,
            умерший под забором,
рядом
      с десятком
                  моих коллег.
Подведите
          мой
              посмертный баланс!
Я утверждаю
            и — знаю — не налгу:
на фоне
        сегодняшних
                    дельцов и пролаз
я буду
      — один! —
                в непролазном долгу.
Долг наш —
            реветь
                    медногорлой сиреной
в тумане мещанья,
                  у бурь в кипеньи.
Поэт
    всегда
          должник вселенной,
платящий
          на го́ре
                  проценты
                          и пени.
Я
  в долгу

                    the sun
                                like a fattened hog
rises
        on a future
                        without beggars and cripples,
I shall
            already
                    be a putrefied corpse
                                        under a fence,
together
            with a dozen
                        of my colleagues.
Draw up
            my
                    posthumous balance!
I hereby declare—
                        and I'm telling no lies:
Among
            today's
                    swindlers and dealers,
I alone
            shall be sunk
                        in hopeless debt.
Our duty is
            to blare
                        like brass-throated horns
in the fogs of bourgeois vulgarity
                                and seething storms.
A poet
        is always
                    indebted to the universe,
paying,
        alas,
            interest
                    and fines.
I am
        indebted

перед Бродвейской лампионией,
перед вами,
                багдадские небеса,
перед Красной Армией,
                        перед вишнями Японии —
перед всем,
        про что
                не успел написать.
А зачем
        вообще
                эта шапка Сене?
Чтобы — целься рифмой
                        и ритмом ярись?
Слово поэта —
                ваше воскресение,
ваше бессмертие,
                гражданин канцелярист.
Через столетья
                в бумажной раме
возьми строку
                и время верни!
И встанет
        день этот
                        с фининспекторами,
с блеском чудес
                и с вонью чернил.
Сегодняшних дней убежденный житель,
выправьте
        в энкапеэс
                        на бессмертье билет
и, высчитав
        действие стихов,
                        разложите
заработок мой
        на триста лет!

        to the lights of the Broadway,
to you,
     to the skies of Bagdadi,[3]
to the Red Army,
        to the cherry trees of Japan—
to everything
     about which
        I have not yet written.
But, after all,
     who needs
       all this stuff?[4]
Is its aim to rhyme
       and rage in rhythm?
No, a poet's word
       is your resurrection
and your immortality,
       citizen and official.
Centuries hence,
     take a line of verse
from its paper frame
       and bring back time!
And this day
     with its tax collectors,
its aura of miracles
       and its stench of ink,
will dawn again.
Convinced dweller in the present day,
go
  to the N.K.P.S.,[5]
       take a ticket to immortality
and, reckoning
     the effect
       of my verse,
stagger my earnings
      over three hundred years!

Но сила поэта
                  не только в этом,
что, вас
          вспоминая,
                      в грядущем икнут.
Нет!
      И сегодня
                  рифма поэта —
ласка
      и лозунг,
                  и штык,
                          и кнут.
Гражданин фининспектор,
                          я выплачу пять,
все
    нули
          у цифры скрестя!
Я
  по праву
            требую пядь
в ряду
        беднейших
                    рабочих и крестьян.
А если
        вам кажется,
                      что всего делóв —
это пользоваться
                  чужими словесами,
то вот вам,
            товарищи,
                      мое стилó,
и можете
          писать
                  сами!

(1926)

But the poet is strong
                    not only because,
remembering you,
            the people of the future
                            will hiccup.[6]
No!
    Nowadays too
                the poet's rhyme
is a caress
            and a slogan,
                    a bayonet
                            and a knout!
Citizen tax collector,
                    I'll cross out
all the zeros
            after the five
                        and pay the rest.
I demand
        as my right
                    an inch of ground
among
        the poorest
                    workers and peasants.
And if
        you think
                that all I have to do
is to profit
            by other people's words,
then,
        comrades,
                    here's my pen.
Take
        a crack at it
                    yourselves!
(1926)

ПИСЬМО ТОВАРИЩУ КОСТРОВУ ИЗ ПАРИЖА О СУЩНОСТИ ЛЮБВИ

Простите
        меня,
                товарищ Костров,
с присущей
        душевной ширью,
что часть
        на Париж отпущенных строф
на лирику
        я
                растранжирю.
Представьте:
        входит
                красавица в зал,
в меха
        и бусы оправленная.
Я
  эту красавицу взял
                и сказал:
— правильно сказал
                или неправильно? —
Я, товарищ, —
                из России,
знаменит в своей стране я,
я видал
        девиц красивей,
я видал
        девиц стройнее.
Девушкам
        поэты любы.
Я ж умен

208

LETTER FROM PARIS TO COMRADE KOSTROV ON THE NATURE OF LOVE[1]

Forgive
        me,
                Comrade Kostrov,
with your usual
                generosity,
for squandering
                on lyrics
                                part
of the lines
                allotted to Paris.
Picture this:
                a beauty
                                all inset in furs
and beads,
                enters a drawing room.
I
  seized this beauty
                and said:
—did I speak right
                or wrong?—
Comrade,
        I come from Russia;
I am famous in my land;
I have seen
                more beautiful girls,
I have seen
                more shapely girls.
Girls are partial
                to poets.
I am clever

и голосист,
заговариваю зубы —
только
            слушать согласись.
Не поймать
                меня
                            на дряни,
на прохожей
                    паре чувств.
Я ж
        навек
                любовью ранен —
еле-еле волочусь.
Мне
        любовь
                не свадьбой мерить:
разлюбила —
                    уплыла.
Мне, товарищ,
                    в высшей мере
наплевать
                на купола.
Что ж в подробности вдаваться,
шутки бросьте-ка,
мне ж, красавица,
                        не двадцать, —
тридцать...
                с хвостиком.
Любовь
        не в том,
                    чтоб кипеть крутей.
нè в том,
        что жгут ýгольями,
а в том,
        что встает за горами грудей

and loudmouthed;
I can talk your head off—
provided
          you agree to listen.
You won't fool
              me
                  by talking cheap,
with a fleeting
                pair of feelings.
Love has inflicted
              on me
                  a lasting wound—
I can barely move.
Marriage
        is no measure
                    of my love:
fallen out of love—
                  she drifted away.
Comrade,
        to hell
with
    cupolas.[2]
But why delve into details?
An end to this joking,
my beauty,
          I am not twenty—
thirty . . .
          and a bit.
Love's sense
            lies not
                    in boiling hotter,
or in being burnt
                  by live coals,
but in what
            rises beyond hilly breasts,

над
     волосами-джунглями.
Любить —
       это значит:
              в глубь двора
вбежать
      и до ночи грачьей,
блестя топором,
          рубить дрова,
силой
    своей
       играючи.
Любить —
      это с простынь,
             бессонницей рваных,
срываться,
      ревнуя к Копернику,
его,
   а не мужа Марьи Иванны,
считая
     своим
       соперником.
Нам
   любовь
      не рай да кущи,
нам
   любовь
      гудит про то,
что опять
    в работу пущен
сердца
    выстывший мотор.
Вы
  к Москве
     порвали нить.

above
      the jungles of hair.
To love
      means this:
            to run
into the depths of a yard
            and, till the rook-black night,
chop wood
      with a shining axe,
giving full play
         to one's
           strength.
To love
      is to break away
           from bedsheets
torn by insomnia,
         jealous of Copernicus,
because he,
      rather than Maria Ivanna's husband,[3]
is
  the true
      rival.
Love
    for us
        is no paradise of arbors—
to us
    love
      tells us, humming,
that the stalled motor
         of the heart
has started to work
        again.
You
    have broken the thread
        to Moscow.

Годы —
          расстояние.
Как бы
      вам бы
            объяснить
это состояние?
На земле
          огней — до неба...
В синем небе
                звезд —
                      до черта.
Если б я
          поэтом нé был,
я бы
    стал бы
              звездочетом.
Подымает площадь шум,
экипажи движутся,
я хожу,
          стишки пишу
в записную книжицу.
Мчат
      авто
          по улице,
а не свалят нáземь.
Понимают
            умницы:
человек —
            в экстазе.
Сонм видений
                и идей
полон
      до крышки.
Тут бы

Years:
>   distance.
How can I
>   explain
>   to you
my state of mind?
The earth
>   has a whole skyful of lights . . .
The blue sky,
>   a hell of a lot
>   of stars.
If I were not
>   a poet,
I would
>   become
>   a stargazer.
Public squares begin to buzz;
carriages roll past;
I stroll about,
>   jotting verse
in my notebook.
Cars
>   whir
>   along the street
without knocking me down.
They understand,
>   the smart fellows:
here is a man
>   in ecstasy.
The assembly of visions
>   and ideas
is brimmed
>   to the lid.
Here

и у медведей
выросли бы крылышки.
И вот
    с какой-то
                грошовой столовой,
когда
    докипело это,
из зева
    до звезд
                взвивается слово
золоторожденной кометой.
Распластан
        хвост
                небесам на треть,
блестит
    и горит оперенье его,
чтоб двум влюбленным
                    на звезды смотреть
из ихней
        беседки сиреневой.
Чтоб подымать,
            и вести,
                    и влечь,
которые глазом ослабли.
Чтоб вражьи
            головы
                спиливать с плеч
хвостатой
        сияющей саблей.
Себя
    до последнего стука в груди,
как на свиданьи,
                простаивая,
прислушиваюсь:

even bears
might grow wings.
And so
            from some
                        fifth-rate restaurant,
when all this
            has boiled over,
from my gullet
            the word soars
                        to the stars
like a golden-born comet.
The tail
            splashes across
                        a third of the sky,
its plumage
            sparkling and burning,
so that a pair of lovers
                        may admire the stars
from their
            lilac-bloomed arbor.
To lift up,
            and lead,
                        and entice,
those who have grown weak in the eye.
To saw from shoulders
                        hostile
                                    heads
with the tail
            of a glittering sword.
Myself—
            to the last heartbeat,
rooted
            as at a lover's meeting—
myself I hear:

любовь загудит —
человеческая,
                простая.
Ураган,
        огонь,
                вода
подступают в ропоте.
Кто
   сумеет
            совладать?
Можете?
        Попробуйте...
(1928)

> love will always hum—
love,
>　　human and simple.
Hurricane,
>　　　　fire,
>　　　　　　water
surge forward, rumbling.
Who
>　　can
>　　　　control this?
Can you?
>　　　　Try it . . .
(1928)

ВО ВЕСЬ ГОЛОС

ПЕРВОЕ ВСТУПЛЕНИЕ В ПОЭМУ.

Уважаемые
            товарищи потомки!
Роясь
     в сегодняшнем
                   окаменевшем говне,
наших дней изучая потемки,
вы ,
   возможно,
               спросите и обо мне.
И, возможно, скажет
                ваш ученый,
кроя эрудицией
              вопросов рой,
что жил-де такой
               певец кипяченой
и ярый враг воды сырой.
Профессор,
          снимите очки-велосипед!
Я сам расскажу
             о времени
                  и о себе.
Я, ассенизатор
           и водовоз,
революцией
           мобилизованный и призванный,
ушел на фронт
           из барских садоводств
поэзии —
         бабы капризной.
Засадила садик мило,

AT THE TOP OF MY VOICE[1]

FIRST PRELUDE TO THE POEM

My most respected
                comrades of posterity!
Rummaging among
            these days'
                  petrified crap,
exploring the twilight of our times,
you,
      possibly,
           will inquire about me too.
And, possibly, your scholars
                will declare,
with their erudition overwhelming
                  a swarm of problems;
once there lived
         a certain champion of boiled water,
and inveterate enemy of raw water.[2]
Professor,
      take off your bicycle glasses!
I myself will expound
             those times
               and myself.
I, a latrine cleaner
         and water carrier,
by the revolution
           mobilized and drafted,
went off to the front
             from the aristocratic gardens
of poetry—
        the capricious wench.
She planted a delicious garden,

дочка,
    дачка,
        водь
           и гладь —
Сама садик я садила,
сама буду поливать.
Кто стихами льет из лейки,
кто кропит,
        набравши в рот, —
кудреватые Митрейки,
           мудреватые Кудрейки —
кто их, к черту, разберет!
Нет на прорву карантина —
мандолинят из-под стен:
«Тара-тина, тара-тина,
т-эн-н...»
Неважная честь,
        чтоб из этаких роз
мои изваяния высились
по скверам,
        где харкает туберкулез,
где бляди с хулиганом
           да сифилис.
И мне
    агитпроп
        в зубах навяз,
и мне бы
    строчить
        романсы на вас —
доходней оно
        и прелестней.
Но я
    себя
        смирял,

222

the daughter,
>> cottage,
>>> pond
>>>> and meadow.

Myself a garden I did plant,
myself with water sprinkled it.[3]
Some pour their verse from water cans;
others spit water
>> from their mouth—
the curly Macks,
>> the clever Jacks—[4]
but what the hell's it all about!
There's no damming all this up—
beneath the walls they mandoline:
"Tara-tina, tara-tine,
tw-a-n-g . . ." [5]
It's no great honor, then,
>>> for my monuments
to rise from such roses
above the public squares,
>>> where consumption coughs,
where whores, hooligans, and syphilis
>>>> walk.

Agitprop[6]
>> sticks
>>> in my teeth too,
and I'd rather
>> compose
>>> romances for you—
more profit in it
>> and more charm.
But I
> subdued
>> myself,

                    становясь
на горло
              собственной песне.
Слушайте,
              товарищи потомки,
агитатора,
              горлана-главаря.
Заглуша
              поэзии потоки,
я шагну
              через лирические томики,
как живой
              с живыми говоря.
Я к вам приду
                    в коммунистическое далеко́
не так,
              как песенно-есененный провитязь.
Мой стих дойдет
                    через хребты веков
и через головы
              поэтов и правительств.
Мой стих дойдет,
                    но он дойдет не так, —
не как стрела
              в амурно-лировой охоте,
не как доходит
                    к нумизмату стершийся пятак
и не как свет умерших звезд доходит.
Мой стих
              трудом
                    громаду лет прорвет
и явится
         весомо,
                 грубо,
                        зримо,
как в наши дни

                    setting my heel
on the throat
                    of my own song.
Listen,
        comrades of posterity,
to the agitator,
                    the rabble-rouser.
Stifling
        the torrents of poetry,
I'll skip
        the volumes of lyrics;
as one alive,
            I'll address the living.
I'll join you
            in the far communist future,
I, who am
            no Esenin super-hero.[7]
My verse will reach you
                    across the peaks of ages,
over the heads
            of governments and poets.
My verse
        will reach you
not as an arrow
            in a cupid-lyred chase,
not as worn penny
            reaches a numismatist,
not as the light of dead stars reaches you.
My verse
        by labor
            will break the mountain chain of years,
and will present itself
                    ponderous,
                            crude,
                                tangible,
as an aqueduct,

вошел водопровод,
сработанный
еще рабами Рима.
В курганах книг,
похоронивших стих,
железки строк случайно обнаруживая,
вы
с уважением
ощупывайте их,
как старое,
но грозное оружие.
Я
ухо
словом
не привык ласкать;
ушку девическому
в завиточках волоска
с полупохабщины
не разалеться тронуту.
Парадом развернув
моих страниц войска,
я прохожу
по строчечному фронту.
Стихи стоят
свинцово-тяжело,
готовые и к смерти
и к бессмертной славе.
Поэмы замерли,
к жерлу прижав жерло
нацеленных
зияющих заглавий.
Оружия
любимейшего род,
готовая
рвануться в гике,

226

by slaves of Rome
constructed,
enters into our days.
When in mounds of books,
where verse lies buried,
you discover by chance the iron filings of lines,
touch them
with respect,
as you would
some antique
yet awesome weapon.
It's no habit of mine
to caress
the ear
with words;
a maiden's ear
curly-ringed
will not crimson
when flicked by smut.
In parade deploying
the armies of my pages,
I shall inspect
the regiments in line.
Heavy as lead,
my verses at attention stand,
ready for death
and for immortal fame.
The poems are rigid,
pressing muzzle
to muzzle their gaping
pointed titles.
The favorite
of all the armed forces,
the cavalry of witticisms,
ready

застыла
       кавалерия острот,
поднявши рифм
            отточенные пики.
И все
       поверх зубов вооруженные войска,
что двадцать лет в победах
                 пролетали,
до самого
       последнего листка
я отдаю тебе,
         планеты пролетарий.
Рабочего
       громады класса враг —
он враг и мой,
         отъявленный и давний.
Велели нам
       идти
          под красный флаг
года труда
        и дни недоеданий.
Мы открывали
         Маркса
           каждый том,
как в доме
        собственном
             мы открываем ставни,
но и без чтения
         мы разбирались в том,
в каком идти,
         в каком сражаться стане.
Мы
  диалектику
         учили не по Гегелю.
Бряцанием боев

to launch a wild hallooing charge,
reins its chargers still,
                              raising
the pointed lances of the rhymes.
And all
            these troops armed to the teeth,
which have flashed by
                              victoriously for twenty years,
all these,
            to their very last page,
I present to you,
                    the planet's proletarian.
The enemy
            of the massed working class
is my enemy too,
                    inveterate and of long standing.
Years of trial
            and days of hunger
                                    ordered us
to march
            under the red flag.
We opened
            each volume
                    of Marx
as we would open
            the shutters
                    in our own house;
but we did not have to read
                    to make up our minds
which side to join,
                    which side to fight on.
Our dialectics
            were not learned
                    from Hegel.
In the roar of battle

она врывалась в стих,
когда
           под пулями
                           от нас буржуи бегали,
как мы
           когда-то
                 бегали от них.
Пускай
      за гениями
                     безутешною вдовой
плетется слава
                 в похоронном марше —
умри, мой стих,
                 умри, как рядовой,
как безымянные
                 на штурмах мерли наши!
Мне наплевать
                 на бронзы многопудье,
мне наплевать
                 на мраморную слизь.
Сочтемся славою —
                   ведь мы свои же люди, —
пускай нам
           общим памятником будет
построенный
           в боях
                   социализм.
Потомки,
      словарей проверьте поплавки:
из Леты
      выплывут
                 остатки слов таких,
как «проституция»,
                 «туберкулез»,
                             «блокада».

                    it erupted into verse,
when,
        under fire,
                    the bourgeois decamped
as once we ourselves
                    had fled
                            from them.
Let fame
        trudge
                after genius
like an inconsolable widow
                            to a funeral march—
die then, my verse,
                die like a common soldier,
like our men
            who nameless died attacking!
I don't care a spit
                for tons of bronze;
I don't care a spit
                for slimy marble.
We're men of a kind,
                we'll come to terms about our fame;
let our
        common monument be
socialism
            built
                in battle.
Men of posterity
                examine the flotsam of dictionaries:
out of Lethe
            will bob up
                        the debris of such words
as "prostitution,"
                "tuberculosis,"
                                "blockade."

Для вас,
        которые
                здоровы и ловки,
поэт
    вылизывал
                чахоткины плевки
шершавым языком плаката.
С хвостом годов
                  я становлюсь подобием
чудовищ
        ископаемо-хвостатых.
Товарищ жизнь,
         давай
                быстрей протопаем,
протопаем
        по пятилетке
                дней остаток.
Мне
    и рубля
             не накопили строчки,
краснодеревщики
                не слали мебель на́ дом.
И кроме
        свежевымытой сорочки,
скажу по совести,
                мне ничего не надо.
Явившись
        в Це Ка Ка
                идущих
                    светлых лет,
над бандой
        поэтических
                рвачей в выжиг
я подыму,

For you,
          who are now
                    healthy and agile,
the poet,
          with the rough tongue
                    of his posters,[8]
has licked away consumptives' spittle.
With the tail of my years behind me,
                         I begin to resemble
those monsters,
          excavated dinosaurs.
Comrade life,
               let us
                    march faster,
march
     faster through what's left
                    of the five-year plan.
My verse
          has brought me
                    no rubles to spare:
no craftsmen have made
                    mahogany chairs for my house.
In all conscience,
               I need nothing
except
     a freshly laundered shirt.
When I appear
          before the CCC [9]
                         of the coming
                              bright years,
by way of my Bolshevik party card,
                         I'll raise
above the heads
          of a gang of self-seeking

как большевистский партбилет,
все сто томов
моих
партийных книжек.

(1930)

                                        poets and rogues,
all the hundred volumes
                      of my
                      communist-committed books.

(1930)

Уже второй. Должно быть, ты легла.
В ночи Млечпуть серебряной Окою.
Я не спешу, и молниями телеграмм
мне незачем тебя будить и беспокоить.
Как говорят, инцидент исперчен.
Любовная лодка разбилась о быт.
С тобой мы в расчете. И не к чему перечень
взаимных болей, бед и обид.
Ты посмотри, какая в мире тишь.
Ночь обложила небо звездной данью.
В такие вот часы встаешь и говоришь
векам, истории и мирозданию.
(1930)

PAST ONE O'CLOCK[1]. . .

Past one o'clock. You must have gone to bed.
The Milky Way streams silver through the night.[2]
I'm in no hurry; with lightning telegrams
I have no cause to wake or trouble you.[3]
And, as they say, the incident is closed.[4]
Love's boat has smashed against the daily grind.
Now you and I are quits. Why bother then
to balance mutual sorrows, pains, and hurts.
Behold what quiet settles on the world.
Night wraps the sky in tribute from the stars.
In hours like these, one rises to address
The ages, history, and all creation.
(1930)

THE BEDBUG

An extravaganza in 9 scenes

Dramatis Personae

IVAN PRISYPKIN (otherwise known as PIERRE SKRIP-
KIN), a former Party member, former worker,
and now the fiancé of

ELZEVIR DAVIDOVNA RENAISSANCE, manicurist and
cashier of a beauty parlor

ROSALIE PAVLOVNA RENAISSANCE, her mother

DAVID OSIPOVICH RENAISSANCE, her father

ZOYA BERYOZKINA, a working girl

OLEG BARD, an eccentric house-owner

MILITIAMAN

PROFESSOR

DIRECTOR OF ZOO

FIRE CHIEF

FIREMEN

USHER AT WEDDING

REPORTER

WORKERS

CHAIRMAN OF CITY SOVIET

ORATOR

HIGH SCHOOL STUDENTS

MASTER OF CEREMONIES

MEMBERS OF PRESIDIUM OF CITY SOVIET, HUNTERS, CHILDREN, OLD PEOPLE

SCENE 1

(1929. Tambov, U.S.S.R. Center: Huge revolving door of State Department Store. Sides: Display windows full of goods. People entering empty-handed and coming out with bundles. Private peddlers[1] walking through the aisles.)

MAN SELLING BUTTONS: Why get married on account of a button? Why get divorced on account of a button? Just press your thumb against your index finger and you won't lose your pants, citizens! Dutch grippers! They sew themselves on! Twenty kopecks for half a dozen!
Here you are, gentlemen!

MAN SELLING DOLLS:
Dancing dolls!
Straight from the ballet studios!
The best toy for indoors and outdoors!
Dances to the order of the People's Commissar!

WOMAN SELLING APPLES:
We ain't got no pineapples!
We ain't got no bananas!
Top-grade apples at fifteen kopecks for four!
Like some, lady?

MAN SELLING WHETSTONES:
Unbreakable German whetstones!
Any one you choose for thirty kopecks!
Hones where you like and how you like!
Sharpens razors, knives—and tongues for political
    discussions!

MAN SELLING LAMPSHADES:
Lampshades! Lampshades!
All sizes and colors!
Blue for comfort and red for passion!
Get yourselves a lampshade, comrades!

MAN SELLING BALLOONS:
Sausage balloons!
Fly like a bird!
Nobile[2] could have used one at the North Pole!
Step right up, citizens!

MAN SELLING SALTED HERRINGS:
Best herrings! Best herrings!
Indispensable with pancakes and vodka!

WOMAN SELLING UNDERWEAR:
Brassieres! Brassieres!
Lovely fur-lined brassieres!

MAN SELLING GLUE:
Why throw out your broken crockery?
Famous Excelsior glue!
Fixes anything from Venus de Milo to a chamber
    pot!
Like to try it, lady?

WOMAN SELLING PERFUME:
Coty perfume by the ounce!
Coty perfume by the ounce!

MAN SELLING BOOKS:
What the wife does when the husband's away!

244

A hundred and five funny stories by the ex-Count
Leo Nikolaevich Tolstoy!
Fifteen kopecks instead of a ruble twenty!

WOMAN SELLING UNDERWEAR:
Lovely brassieres!
Fur-lined brassieres!

(*Enter* PRISYPKIN, ROSALIE PAVLOVNA, *and* OLEG
BARD.)

PRISYPKIN (*excitedly*): Look at those aristocratic
bonnets!

ROSALIE: They're not bonnets, they're . . .

PRISYPKIN: Think I'm blind? Suppose we have
twins? There'll be one for Dorothy and one for
Lillian when they go out walking together. . . .
That's what I'm going to call them: Dorothy and
Lillian—aristocratic—like the Gish sisters. Now
you buy those bonnets, Rosalie . . . my house
must be like a horn of plenty.

OLEG BARD (*giggling*): Buy 'em, buy 'em, Rosalie
Pavlovna! He doesn't mean to be vulgar—that's
how the up-and-coming working class sees things.
Here he is, bringing an immaculate proletarian
origin and a union card into your family and you
count your kopecks! His house must be like a horn
of plenty.

(ROSALIE *buys with a sigh.*)

OLEG BARD: Let me carry them—they're quite light. Don't worry—it won't cost you any more. . . .

MAN SELLING TOYS: Dancing dolls from the ballet studios. . . .

PRISYPKIN: My future children must be brought up refined. There, buy one, Rosalie Pavlovna!

ROSALIE PAVLOVNA: Comrade Prisypkin. . . .

PRISYPKIN: Don't call me comrade! You're not a proletarian yet—not till after the marriage!

ROSALIE PAVLOVNA: Well, *Mister* Prisypkin, for this money fifteen men could have a shave—beards, whiskers, and all. What about an extra dozen beers for the wedding instead?

PRISYPKIN (*sternly*): Rosalie Pavlovna, my house must be filled like a horn. . . .

OLEG BARD: His house must be like a horn of plenty. Beer must flow like a river, and dancing dolls, too —like out of a cornucopia.

(ROSALIE PAVLOVNA *buys*.)

OLEG BARD (*seizing the parcels*): Don't worry—it won't cost you any more.

MAN SELLING BUTTONS:
Why get married on account of a button?
Why get divorced on account of a button?

PRISYPKIN: In our Red family there must be no petty bourgeois squabbles over fly buttons. There we are! Buy them, Rosalie Pavlovna!

OLEG BARD: Rosalie Pavlovna, don't provoke him until you get that union card. He is the victorious class and he sweeps away everything in his path, like lava, and Comrade Prisypkin's pants must be like a horn of plenty. . . .

(ROSALIE PAVLOVNA *buys with a sigh.*)

OLEG BARD: Allow me . . . I'll take them and it won't cost you. . . .

MAN SELLING SALTED HERRINGS: Finest republican herrings!
Indispensable with every kind of vodka!

ROSALIE PAVLOVNA (*brightening, pushing everybody aside, loudly*): Yes! salted herrings! Now that's something for the wedding, I'll sure take some of them. Let me through, sir! How much is this sardine?

MAN SELLING SALTED HERRINGS: This salmon costs two-sixty the kilo.

ROSALIE PAVLOVNA: Two-sixty for that overgrown minnow?

MAN SELLING SALTED HERRINGS: Really, madam! Only two-sixty for this budding sturgeon!

ROSALIE PAVLOVNA: Two-sixty for these marinated corset stays! Did you hear that, Comrade Skripkin? Oh, how right you were to kill the Tsar and drive out Mr. Ryabushinsky! [3] Oh, the bandits! I shall claim my civic rights and buy my herrings in the Soviet State Co-op!

OLEG BARD: Wait a moment, Comrade Skripkin. Why get mixed up with petty bourgeois elements and haggle over herrings like this? Give me fifteen rubles and a bottle of vodka and I'll fix you up with a wedding in a million.

PRISYPKIN: Comrade Bard, I'm against all this petty bourgeois stuff—lace curtains and canaries . . . I'm a man with higher needs. What I'm interested in is a wardrobe with a mirror. . . .

(ZOYA BERYOZKINA *nearly runs into them as they stand talking. Steps back in astonishment and listens.*)

OLEG BARD: When your cortege . . .

PRISYPKIN: What's that? Some kind of card-game?

OLEG BARD: Cortege, I say. That's what they call processions of all kinds, particularly wedding processions, in these lovely foreign languages.

PRISYPKIN: Well, what do you know!

OLEG BARD: As I was saying, when the cortege advances I'll sing you the epithalamium of Hymen.

248

PRISYPKIN: Huh? What's that about the Himalayas?

OLEG BARD: Not the Himalayas . . . an epithalamium about the god Hymen. That was a god these Greeks had. I mean the ancient republican Greeks, not these mad-dog guttersnipe opportunists like Venizelos.

PRISYPKIN: What I want for my money is a real Red wedding and no gods! Get it?

OLEG BARD: Why, of course, Comrade Skripkin! Not only do I understand, but by virtue of that power of imagination which, according to Plekhanov,[4] is granted to Marxists, I can already see as through a prism, so to speak, the triumph of your class as symbolized by your sublime, ravishing, elegant, and class-conscious wedding! The bride steps out of her carriage and she's all red—that is, she's all steamed up. And leading her by the arm is her red escort, Yerikalov, the bookkeeper—he's fat, red, and apoplectic . . . and you are brought in by the red ushers, the table is covered with red hams, and the bottles all have red seals.

PRISYPKIN (approvingly): That's it! That's it!

OLEG BARD: The red guests shout "Kiss, kiss!"[5] and your red spouse puts her red lips to yours. . . .

ZOYA BERYOZKINA (seizes both of them by the arms; they remove her hands and dust off their sleeves): Vanya! What's he talking about, this catfish in a cravat? What wedding? Who's getting married?

249

OLEG BARD: The Red nuptials of Elzevir Davidovna Renaissance and . . .

PRISYPKIN:
I love another, Zoya,
She's smarter and cuter
With a bosom held tighter
By a beautiful sweater

ZOYA BERYOZKINA: But what about me, Vanya? Who do you think you are? A sailor with a girl in every port?

PRISYPKIN (*wards her off with outstretched hand*): "We part like ships in the sea . . ."

ROSALIE PAVLOVNA (*rushing from the shop, holding a herring above her head*): Whales! Dolphins! (*To the herring peddler.*) Now then, show me that snail! (*she compares. The street-vendor's herrings are larger. Wrings her hands*) Longer by a tail's length! What did we fight for, Comrade Skripkin, eh? Why, oh, why did we kill the Tsar? Why did we throw out Mr. Ryabushinsky? This Soviet regime of yours will drive me to my grave. . . . A whole tail's length longer!

OLEG BARD: My dear Rosalie Pavlovna, try comparing them at the other end. They're only bigger by a head and what do you want the heads for? You can't eat them and you'll cut them off and throw them out anyway.

ROSALIE PAVLOVNA: Did you hear that? If I cut off your head, Comrade Bard, it will be no loss to anyone, but if I cut off these herrings' heads I lose ten kopecks to the kilo. Well, let's go home. . . . I sure want a union card in the family, but my daughter's in a good business, and that's nothing to sniff at!

ZOYA BERYOZKINA: We were going to live and work together . . . so it's all over. . . .

PRISYPKIN: Our love is liquidated. I'll call the militia if you interfere with my freedom of love as a citizen.

ROSALIE PAVLOVNA: What does she want, this slut? Why have you got your hooks on my son-in-law?

ZOYA BERYOZKINA: He's mine!

ROSALIE PAVLOVNA: Ah! She's pregnant! I'll pay her off, but I'll smash her face in first!

MILITIAMAN: Citizens! Stop this disgusting behavior!

SCENE 2

(*Hostel for young workers.* INVENTOR *huffs and puffs over a blueprint.* YOUTH *lolls around.* GIRL *sits on the edge of the bed.* YOUTH IN SPECTACLES *with nose buried in a book. Whenever the door opens, a long corridor with doors off and light-bulbs is seen.*)

BAREFOOT YOUTH (*howling at the top of his voice*): Where are my boots? Someone's swiped my boots again! Am I supposed to check them every night in the baggage room at the Kursk Station? Is that what I've got to do? Is that it?

CLEANER: Prisypkin took them to go see his lady-love, his she-camel. He cursed while he put them on. "This is the last time," he said. "In the evening," he said, "I shall present myself in a get-up more appropriate to my new social status."

YOUTH: The bastard!

YOUNG WORKER (*tidying up the room*): The trash he leaves behind him is kind of more refined now-adays. It used to be empty beer-bottles and fish-tails and now it's cologne bottles and ties all the colors of the rainbow.

GIRL: Shut your trap! The kid buys a new tie and you curse him like he was Ramsay MacDonald.

YOUTH: That's just what he is—Ramsay MacDonald! The new tie don't matter. Trouble is that he's tied to the tie—not the tie to him. He don't even use his head any more, so his tie shouldn't get twisted.

CLEANER: If there's a hole in his sock and he's in a hurry, he paints it over with indelible ink.

YOUTH: His feet are black anyway.

INVENTOR: But maybe not black in the places where the holes are. He ought to just switch his socks from one foot to the other.

CLEANER: There's the inventor for you! Why don't you take out a patent before somebody steals the idea?

(*Whisks a duster over the table, upsets a box from which visiting-cards drop out fanwise. Bends down to pick them up, holds them to the light, laughs so hard he can barely manage to motion his comrades toward him.*)

ALL (*reading and repeating after each other*): Pierre Skripkin! [1] Pierre Skripkin!

INVENTOR: That's the name he's invented for himself. Prisypkin. Who is Prisypkin? What good's Prisypkin? What's the point of Prisypkin? But Pierre Skripkin—that's not a name, it's a romance!

GIRL (*dreamily*): But it's true! Pierre Skripkin is very fine and elegant. You roar your heads off but how do you know he's not carrying out a cultural revolution in his own home?

YOUTH: Yeah, Pushkin's got nothing on him with those sideburns of his. They hang down like a pair of dog's tails and he doesn't even wash them to keep them neat.

GIRL: There's that movie star with sideburns. . . .

INVENTOR: Prisypkin got the idea from him.

YOUTH: And what does his hero's hair grow on, I'd like to know? He's got no head at all, but a whole halo of fuzz. Wonder what makes it grow? Must be the dampness.

YOUTH WITH BOOK: Anyway, he's no movie star. . . . He's a writer. I don't know what he's written, but I know he's famous! They've written about him three times in *Evening Moscow*: they say that he sold Apukhtin's[2] poetry as his own, and Apukhtin got so mad he wrote a denial. And so what's-his-name came back and said: "You're all crazy, it's not true, I copied it from Nadson." [3] I don't know which of them is lying. It's true they don't print him any more, but he's very famous. He gives lessons to young people—how to write verse, how to dance, and, well, you know . . . how to borrow money.

YOUTH WITH BROOM: Painting over holes with ink —that's no way for a worker to behave!

(MECHANIC, *grease-covered, comes in halfway through this sentence. Washes his hands and turns around.*)

MECHANIC: He's no worker. He quit his job today. He's marrying a young lady—a hairdresser's daughter. She's the cashier and the manicurist too. Mademoiselle Elzevir Renaissance'll clip his claws for him now. . . .

INVENTOR: Elzevir—that's the name of a type face.

MECHANIC: I don't know about her type face, but she's certainly got a figure! He showed her picture to our payclerk today . . .
What a honey, what a peach—
Both her breasts weigh eighty pounds each!

BAREFOOT YOUTH: He's sure fixed himself up!

GIRL: Jealous, eh?

BAREFOOT YOUTH: So what? When I get to be foreman and earn enough to buy myself a pair of boots, I'll start looking around for a cozy little apartment.

MECHANIC: Here's my advice to you: get yourself some curtains. You can either open them and look out at the street or close them and take your bribes in private. It's better to work with other people, but it's much more fun to eat your sirloin by yourself. Right? We had men who tried to run away from the trenches, too, and we just swatted them down like flies. Well, why don't you just get out?

BAREFOOT YOUTH: Okay. Okay. Who do you think you are? Karl Liebknecht? [4] If a dame gives you the

255

glad eye out of a window, I bet you fall for it, too, hero!

MECHANIC: I'm no deserter. You think I like wearing these lousy rags? Like hell I do! There are lots of us, you know, and there just aren't enough Nepmen's[5] daughters to go around. . . . We'll build houses for everybody! But we won't creep out of this foxhole with a white flag.

BAREFOOT YOUTH: You and your trenches! This isn't 1919. People want to live their own lives now.

MECHANIC: Well, isn't it like the trenches in here?

BAREFOOT YOUTH: Nuts!

MECHANIC: Look at the lice!

BAREFOOT YOUTH: Nuts!

MECHANIC: Our enemies attack silently now—that's the only difference. And people shoot with noiseless powder!

BAREFOOT YOUTH: Nuts!

MECHANIC: Look at Prisypkin—he's been shot by a two-eyed, double-barreled gun!

(*Enter* PRISYPKIN *in patent leather shoes. In one hand he holds a pair of worn-out shoes by the laces and tosses them over to* BAREFOOT YOUTH. OLEG BARD *carries his purchases. He stands between* PRISYPKIN *and the* MECHANIC, *who is dancing a jig.*)

OLEG BARD: Don't pay any attention to this vulgar dance, Comrade Skripkin, it will only spoil the refined taste that is awakening in you.

(*The youths in the hostel turn their backs.*)

MECHANIC: Quit bowing and scraping. You'll crack your skull.

OLEG BARD: I understand, Comrade Skripkin! You are too sensitive for this vulgar crew. But don't lose your patience for just one more lesson. The first foxtrot after the nuptial ceremonies is a crucial step—it should leave a deathless impression. Well now, take a few steps with an imaginary lady. . . . Why are you stamping your feet like at a May Day parade?

PRISYPKIN: Comrade Bard, let me take my shoes off: they pinch and besides they'll wear out.

OLEG BARD: That's the way! That's right! Tread softly like you were coming back from a saloon on a moonlit night, full of sadness and dreams. That's the way! But don't wriggle your hind-parts! You're supposed to be leading your partner, not driving a pushcart. . . . That's the way! . . . Where's your hand? Your hand's too low!

PRISYPKIN (*passes his hand over an imaginary shoulder*): It won't stay up!

OLEG BARD: And now, Comrade Skripkin, you discreetly locate the lady's brassiere, hook your thumb into it, and rest your hand—it's pleasant for the

257

lady and makes it easier for you. Then you can think about your other hand. . . . Why are you rolling your shoulders? That's not a foxtrot. You're giving a demonstration of the shimmy.

PRISYPKIN: No, I was just scratching myself.

OLEG BARD: That's not the way to do it, Comrade Skripkin! If any such emergency occurs while you're carried away by the dance, roll your eyes, as if you were jealous of the lady, step back to the wall in the Spanish manner, and rub yourself rapidly against some statue or other. In the smart society where you'll be moving there's always a hell of a lot of statues and vases. So rub yourself, screw up your face, flash your eyes, and say: "I understand, tr-r-reacherous one, you are playing a game with me. . . ." Then you start dancing again and pretend you're gradually calming down and cooling off.

PRISYPKIN: Like this?

OLEG BARD: Bravo! Well done! How clever you are, Comrade Skripkin! A man of such talents just doesn't have elbow room in Russia, what with capitalist encirclement and the building of socialism in one country. I ask you—is Lower Goat Street a worthy scene for your activities? You need a world revolution, you must break through into Europe. Once you've smashed the Chamberlains, the Poincarés, you will delight the Moulin Rouge and the Pantheon with the beauty of your bodily movements. Just remember that! Now hold it!

Hold it! Magnificent! But I must be off. I have to keep an eye on the ushers. I'll give them one glass in advance before the wedding and not a drop more. When they've done their job, they can drink straight out of the bottle, if they like. *Au revoir!* (*Shouts from the doorway as he leaves.*) And don't put on two ties at once—particularly if they're different colors. And remember, you can't wear a starched shirt outside your pants!

(PRISYPKIN *tries on his new clothes.*)

YOUTH: Vanya, why don't you cut it out?

PRISYPKIN: Mind your own goddamn business! respected comrade. What did I fight for? I fought for the good life, and now I've got it right here in my hands—a wife, a home, and real etiquette. I'll do my duty, if need be, but it's only we who held the bridgehead who have a right to rest by the river! So there! Mebbe I can raise the standards of the whole proletariat by looking after my own comforts. So there!

MECHANIC: There's a warrior for you! A real Suvorov! [6] Bravo!
For a while I worked my best
Building a bridge to Socialism
But before I was through I wanted a rest
By the bridge to Socialism.
Now it's grown with grass that's grazed by sheep
And all I do is lie and sleep
By the bridge to Socialism.
So that's it, eh?

PRISYPKIN: Leave me alone with your cheap propaganda ditties . . .

(*Sits down on bed and sings to guitar.*)

On Lunacharsky Street
There's an old house I know
With stairs broad and neat
And a most elegant window.

(*A shot. All rush to the door.*)

YOUTH (*from the doorway*): Zoya Beryozkina's shot herself! They'll give her hell for this at the Party meeting!

VOICES:
Help!
First aid!
Help!
First aid!

A VOICE (*on the phone*): First aid! Help! What? She's shot herself! Right through the breast! This is Lower Goat Street, number sixteen.

(PRISYPKIN *alone. Hurriedly collects his belongings.*)

MECHANIC: And a woman like that shoots herself on account of you, you hairy skunk!

(*Grabs* PRISYPKIN *by the jacket and throws him out of the room, hurling his belongings after him.*)

260

CLEANER (*running in with doctor; jerks* PRISYPKIN *to his feet and gives him his hat, which has fallen off*): You're walking out on your class with a hell of a bang!

PRISYPKIN (*turns away and yells*): Cab! Seventeen Lunacharsky Street—and my luggage!

SCENE 3

(Huge beauty parlor. Mirrors decorated with paper flowers. Liquor bottles on small shaving tables. On the left a grand piano with gaping maw. On the right a coal stove whose pipes climb all around the walls. In the middle of the room a banquet table at which sit PIERRE SKRIPKIN, ELZEVIR RENAISSANCE, *the* BEST MAN *(an accountant) and the* MATRON OF HONOR *(accountant's wife).* OLEG BARD *is master of ceremonies and sits in the center of the table.)*

ELZEVIR: Shall we begin, Skrippy, my pet?

PRISYPKIN: Just a minute.

ELZEVIR: Skrippy darling, shall we start?

PRISYPKIN: Wait. I said I wished to get wed in an organized fashion—in the presence of the guests of honor, and particularly in the presence of the secretary of our factory committee, respected Comrade Lassalchenko. . . . Here we are!

GUEST *(running in)*: My dear bride and bridegroom, please forgive me for being late and allow me to convey to you the congratulations of our respected leader, Comrade Lassalchenko. "Tomorrow," he says, "I would even go to the church, if need be, but today," he says, "I can't make it. Today," he says, "is a Party meeting, and like it or not, I have to go to the Party cell. . . ." So let us proceed to current business, as the saying goes.

PRISYPKIN: I hereby declare the wedding open.

ROSALIE PAVLOVNA: Comrades and *Messieurs!* Please eat! Where would you find pigs like these nowadays? I bought this ham three years ago in case of a war with Greece or Poland. . . . But there's still no war and the ham is getting moldy. . . . Eat, gentlemen!

ALL (*raising their glasses*): Kiss! Kiss! [1] (ELZEVIR *and* PIERRE *kiss.*) Kiss! Kiiii-ss-ss!

(ELZEVIR *throws herself around* PIERRE's *neck and he kisses her staidly, conscious of his working-class dignity.*)

BEST MAN: Let's have some Beethoven! Shakespeare! Give us a show! What do they think we celebrate their anniversaries for!

(*The piano is dragged to center of stage.*)

VOICES: By the side! Grab it by the side! Look at its teeth—makes you want to smash them in!

PRISYPKIN: Don't trample on the legs of my piano!

OLEG BARD (*stands up, staggers, and spills his glass*): I am happy, I am happy to see, as we are gathered here today, that the road of Comrade Skripkin's fighting career has come to such a splendid conclusion. It's true that along that road he lost his Party card, but, on the other hand, he did acquire many state lottery tickets. We have succeeded in reconciling, in co-ordinating the couple's class and

263

other contradictions. We who are armed with the Marxist vision cannot fail to see, as in a drop of water, so to speak, the future happiness of humanity—or as it is called in popular parlance: socialism.

ALL: Kiss! Kiss!

(ELZEVIR *and* PRISYPKIN *kiss*.)

OLEG BARD: What gigantic steps we are making on the road to the rebuilding of family life! When we all lay dying at the battle of Perekop,[2] and when many of us, indeed, did die, could we have foreseen that such fragrant roses would blossom forth in this day and age? Could we have imagined, when we groaned under the yoke of autocracy, could even our great teachers Marx and Engels have imagined in their dreams, or dreamed in their imaginations that the bonds of Hymen would one day join together Labor—obscure but grandiose—and Capital—dethroned but ever enchanting?

ALL: Kiss! Kiss!

OLEG BARD: Respected comrades! Beauty is the motive force of progress! What would I have been as a simple worker? Botchkin[3]—just plain Botchkin! What could Botchkin do except bray like an ass? But as Oleg the Bard I can do anything you like! For instance:
I'm Oleg the bard
A happy drunkard
And so now I'm Oleg Bard and enjoy all the bless-

ings of culture as an equal member of society. And I swear—well, no swearing here—but at least I can talk like an ancient Greek:
Prithee, give me, Elzevir
A herring and a glass of beer!
And the whole country responds, just like they were troubadours:
Here's to you, Oleg dear,
A herring's tail and a glass of beer,
To whet your whistle
In style and good cheer!

ALL: Bravo! Hurray! Kiss!

OLEG BARD: Beauty is pregnant with . . .

USHER (*jumps up, menacingly*): Pregnant? Who said "pregnant"? I'll ask you to watch your language in the presence of the newlyweds!

(USHER *is dragged off.*)

ALL: Give us Beethoven! Give us the Kamarinsky! [4]

(OLEG BARD *is dragged to the piano.*)

OLEG BARD:
The tramcars drew up to the Registry Office
Bringing the guests to a Red marriage service. . . .

ALL (*singing in chorus*):
Dressed in his working clothes was the spouse
And a union card stuck out of his blouse!

265

ACCOUNTANT: I get the idea! I get the whole thing!
Hail to thee, Oleg Bardkin
Curly-headed like a lambkin. . . .

HAIRDRESSER (*poking his fork at the* MATRON OF HONOR): No, madam, no! Nobody has curly hair now, after the Revolution! Do you know how we make a *chignon gaufré?* You take the curling iron (*he twists his fork*), heat it on a low flame—*à l'étoile*—(*thrusts his fork into the blazing stove*) and then you whip up a kind of *soufflé* of hair on the crown of the head . . . like this.

MATRON OF HONOR: You insult my honor as a mother and a virgin. . . . Leave me alone, son of a bitch!!!

USHER: Who said "son of a bitch"? I'll ask you to watch your language in the presence of the newly-weds!

(*The* ACCOUNTANT *separates them and continues his song, turning the handle of the cash register as though it were a barrel organ.*)

ELZEVIR (*to* OLEG BARD): Ah, play us the waltz "Makarov's Lament for Vera Kholodnaya". . . .[5] Ah, it's so *charmant;* it's simply a *petite histoire.* . . .

USHER (*armed with a guitar*): Who said *"pissoir"?* I'll ask you to watch . . .

(OLEG BARD *separates them and pounces on the piano keys.*)

USHER (*looks over his shoulder, threateningly*): Why do you play only on the black keys? I suppose you think black is good enough for the proletariat. You play on all the keys only for the bourgeoisie, is that it?

OLEG BARD: Please, citizen, please! I'm concentrating on the white ones!

USHER: So you think white is best? Play on both!

OLEG BARD: I *am* playing on both!

USHER: So you compromise with the Whites,[6] opportunist!

OLEG BARD: But, comrade . . . the keyboard is . . .

USHER: Who said "broad"? And in the presence of the newlyweds! Take that!

(*Hits him on the back of the neck with guitar. The* HAIRDRESSER *sticks his fork into the* MATRON OF HONOR's *hair.* PRISYPKIN *pushes the* ACCOUNTANT *away from his wife.*)

PRISYPKIN: What do you mean by sticking a fish into my wife's breast? This is a bosom, not a flower bed, and that's a fish, not a chrysanthemum!

ACCOUNTANT: And who gave us salmon to eat? You did, huh? So what are you screaming about, huh?

267

(In the tussle the bride is pushed onto the stove. The stove overturns. Her wedding veil catches fire. Flames. Smoke.)

VOICES: We're on fire! . . . Who said "on fire"? . . . Salmon! . . . "The tramcars drew up to the Registry Office. . . ."

SCENE 4

(A fireman's helmet gleams in the darkness, reflecting the light of a nearby fire. Firemen rush on stage, report to their CHIEF *and exit.)*

FIRST FIREMAN: We can't control it, Comrade Chief! We weren't called for two hours . . . the drunken swine! It's burning like a powder magazine. (*Exit.*)

CHIEF: No wonder it burns—cobwebs and liquor.

SECOND FIREMAN: It's dying down . . . the water's turning to icicles. The cellar looks like a skating rink. (*Exit.*)

CHIEF: Found any bodies?

THIRD FIREMAN: One with a smashed skull—must have been hit by a falling beam. Sent it straight to the morgue. (*Exit.*)

FOURTH FIREMAN: One charred corpse of undetermined sex with a fork in its hand.

FIRST FIREMAN: An ex-woman found under the stove with a wire crown on her head.

THIRD FIREMAN: One person unknown of prewar build with a cash register in his hands. Must have been a bandit.

SECOND FIREMAN: No survivors . . . one person un-accounted-for—since the corpse has not been found, I assume it must have burned up entirely.

FIRST FIREMAN: Look at the fireworks! Just like a theater, except that all the actors have been burned up!

THIRD FIREMAN:
They were driven from the marriage
In a Red Cross carriage. . . .

(*A bugler summons the* FIREMEN. *They form ranks and march through the aisles of the theater reciting.*)

FIREMEN:
Comrades and citizens!
                              vodka is toxic!
Drunks can easily
                         burn up the Republic!
A primus stove or an open fire
                    can turn your home into a funeral pyre!
You can start a fire
                           if you chance to doze off
So no bedside reading
                         of Nadson and Zharoff! [1]

SCENE 5

(*Fifty years later. An immense amphitheater for conferences. Instead of human voters, radio loudspeakers equipped with arms like directional signals on an automobile. Above each loudspeaker, colored electric lights. Just below the ceiling there are movie screens. In the center of the hall a dais with a microphone, flanked by control panels and switches for sound and light. Two technicians—an* OLD MAN *and a* YOUTH—*are tinkering around in the darkened hall.*)

OLD MAN (*flicking dust from loudspeakers with a bedraggled feather duster*): It's an important vote today. Check up on the voting apparatus of the agricultural zones and give it a spot of oil. There was a hitch last time. . . .

YOUTH: The agricultural zones? Okay! I'll oil the central zones and polish up the throat of the Smolensk apparatus—they were a bit hoarse again last week. I must tighten up the arms on the metropolitan auxiliary personnel—they're deviating a bit—the right arm tangles with the left one.

OLD MAN: The Ural factories are ready. We'll switch in the Kursk metal works—they've just installed a new apparatus of sixty-two thousand votes for the second group of Zaporozhe power stations. It's pretty good and doesn't give any trouble.

YOUTH: And you remember how it was in the old days? Must have been queer, wasn't it?

OLD MAN: My mother once carried me to a meeting in her arms. There weren't many people—only about a thousand. They were just sitting there, the parasites, and listening. It was some important motion and it was passed by a majority of one. My mother was against it but she couldn't vote because she was holding me in her arms.

YOUTH: Yes . . . That was amateur stuff, of course!

OLD MAN: Apparatus like this wouldn't even have been any good in the old days. A fellow used to have to raise his hand to draw attention to himself —he'd thrust it right in the chairman's face, put both his hands right under his nose. He could have used twelve hands like the ancient god Isis. And lots of people avoided voting. They tell a story about one fellow who sat out some important discussion in the men's room—he was too frightened to vote. He just sat and thought, trying to save his skin.

YOUTH: And did he?

OLD MAN: I'll say he did! But they appointed him to another job. Seeing how much he liked the men's room they put him there permanently in charge of the soap and towels. . . . Everything ready?

YOUTH: Everything!

(*They run down to the control panels. A man with glasses and beard flings open the door and walks straight to the rostrum. Standing with his back to the auditorium, he raises both hands.*)

ORATOR: Plug in all the zones of the Federation!

OLD MAN *and* YOUTHS: Okay!

(*All the red, green, and blue bulbs light up simultaneously.*)

ORATOR: Hello, hello! This is the President of the Institute for Human Resurrection. The motion has been circulated by telegram and has been discussed. The question is clear and simple. At the corner of 62nd Street and 17th Avenue in the former town of Tambov a building brigade, while excavating at a depth of seven meters, has discovered a caved-in, ice-filled cellar. A frozen human figure is visible through the ice. In the opinion of the Institute this individual, who froze to death fifty years ago, could be resurrected. Let us regulate the difference of opinions!

The Institute considers that the life of every worker must be utilized until the very last second.

An X-ray examination has shown that the hands of the individual are callused. Half a century ago calluses were the distinguishing mark of a worker. And let me remind you that after the wars that swept over the world, after the civil wars that led to the creation of our World Federation, human life was declared inviolable by the decree of November 7th, 1965. I have to bring to your attention the objections of the Epidemological Office, which fears a spread of the bacteria known to have infected the former inhabitants of what was once Russia.

In putting the question to the vote, I am fully aware of my responsibility. Comrades, remember, remember, and once again remember:

We are voting

for a human life!

(The lights are dimmed, a high-pitched bell rings. The text of the motion is flashed onto a screen and read out by the ORATOR.*)*

"For the sake of research into the labor habits of the proletariat, for the sake of comparative studies in human life and manners, we demand resurrection!"

(VOICES *from half the loudspeakers: "Quite right! Adopted!" Some other* VOICES: *"Rejected!" The* VOICES *trail off and the screen darkens. A second bell. A new motion is flashed onto the screen and the* ORATOR *reads it out.*)

"Moved by the sanitary-inspection stations of the metallurgical and chemical enterprises of the Don Basin: In view of the danger of the spread of the bacteria of arrogance and sycophancy, which were epidemic in 1929, we demand that the exhibit remain in its refrigerated state."

(VOICES *from the loudspeakers: "Rejected." A few shouts of "Adopted."*)

ORATOR: Any further motions or amendments?

(*Another screen lights up and the* ORATOR *reads from it.*)

"The agricultural zones of Siberia request that the resurrection be postponed until the fall—until the termination of work in the fields—in order to make possible the presence of the broad masses of the people."

(*Overwhelming majority of loudspeakers: "Rejected!" The bulbs light up.*)

I put it to a vote. All in favor of the first motion please raise their hands!

(*Overwhelming majority of the steel hands are raised.*)

Who is in favor of the amendment from Siberia?

(*Two lone hands are raised.*)

The Assembly of the Federation accepts the motion in favor of RE-SUR-RECTION!

(*Roar from all the loudspeakers: "Hurrah!" The* VOICES *die away.*)

The session is closed!

(REPORTERS *rush in through swinging doors. The* ORATOR *cannot restrain himself and shouts joyfully.*)

Resurrection it is! Resurrection! Resurrection!

(The REPORTERS *pull microphones from their pockets.)*

FIRST REPORTER: Hello! 472.5 kilocycles calling. . . . *Eskimo Izvestia.* . . . Resurrection!

SECOND REPORTER: Hello! Hello! 376 kilocycles. . . . *Vitebsk Evening Pravda.* . . . Resurrection!

THIRD REPORTER: Hello! Hello! Hello! 211 kilocycles. . . . *Warsaw Komsomol Pravda.* . . . Resurrection!

FOURTH REPORTER: *Armavir Literary Weekly.* . . . Hello! Hello!

FIFTH REPORTER: Hello! Hello! Hello! . . . 44 kilocycles. . . . *Izvestia of Chicago Soviet.* . . . Resurrection!

SIXTH REPORTER: Hello! Hello! Hello! . . . 115 kilocycles. . . . *Red Gazette of Rome.* . . . Resurrection!

SEVENTH REPORTER: Hello! Hello! Hello! . . . 78 kilocycles. . . . *Shanghai Pauper.* . . . Resurrection!

EIGHTH REPORTER: Hello! Hello! Hello! . . . 220 kilocycles. . . . *Madrid Dairy-Maid.* . . . Resurrection!

NINTH REPORTER: Hello! Hello! . . . 11 kilocycles. . . . *Kabul Pioneer.* . . . Resurrection!

(Newsboys burst in with newssheets fresh from the press.)

FIRST NEWSBOY:
Read how the man froze
Lead stories in verse and prose!

SECOND NEWSBOY:
World-wide poll on number one question!
Can obsequiousness spread by infection?

THIRD NEWSBOY:
Feature on ancient guitars and romances
And other means of drugging the masses!

FOURTH NEWSBOY:
Interview! Interview! Read all about it!

FIFTH NEWSBOY:
Complete list of so-called "dirty words."
Don't be scared, keep your nerve!

SIXTH NEWSBOY:
Science Gazette! Science Gazette!
Theoretical discussion of ancient problem—
Can an elephant die from a cigarette?

SEVENTH NEWSBOY:
It'll make you cry
                  and give you colic—
Explanation of
            the word "alcoholic"!

SCENE 6

(*Sliding door of frosted glass behind which gleam metal parts of surgical apparatus. In front of it are an old* PROFESSOR *and his elderly assistant, who is recognizable as* ZOYA BERYOZKINA. *Both are in white hospital gowns.*)

ZOYA BERYOZKINA: Comrade! Comrade professor! Don't do this experiment, I beg you! Comrade professor, that awful business will start all over again. . . .

PROFESSOR: Comrade Beryozkina, you have begun to live in the past and you talk an incomprehensible language. Just like a dictionary of obsolete words. What's "business"? (*Looks it up in the dictionary*) Business . . . business . . . bootlegger . . . Bulgakov . . . bureaucracy . . . ah, here we are: "business: a kind of activity that prevented every other kind of activity". . . .

ZOYA BERYOZKINA: Well, this "activity" nearly cost me my life fifty years ago. . . . I even went so far as to attempt suicide. . . .

PROFESSOR: Suicide? What's "suicide"? (*looks in dictionary*) . . . supertax . . . surrealism . . . here we are: "suicide." (*Surprised.*) You shot yourself? By a court order? A revolutionary tribunal?

ZOYA BERYOZKINA: No . . . by myself. . . .

PROFESSOR: By yourself? Carelessness?

278

ZOYA BERYOZKINA: No . . . love. . . .

PROFESSOR: Nonsense! Love should make you build bridges and bear children. . . . But you . . . my-my-my!

ZOYA BERYOZKINA: Let me go; I simply can't face it!

PROFESSOR: That really is . . . what was the word? . . . "a business." My-my-my! A business! Society needs you. You must bring all your feelings into play so as to enable this being, whom we are about to unfreeze, to recover from his fifty anazooic years with the maximum of ease. Yes, upon my word! Your presence is very, very important! . . . He and she—that's you I mean! Tell me, were his eyelashes brittle? They might break during the process of rapid defrigeration.

ZOYA BERYOZKINA: Comrade professor, how can I remember eyelashes of fifty years ago!

PROFESSOR: Fifty years ago . . . that was yesterday! And how do you think I manage to remember the color of the hairs on the tail of a mastodon that died half a million years ago? My-my-my! Well, do you remember whether he dilated his nostrils very much while breathing in a state of excitement?

ZOYA BERYOZKINA: Comrade professor, how can I remember? It's thirty years since people dilated their nostrils under such conditions.

PROFESSOR: Well, well, well! And do you have information about the size of his stomach and liver?

—in case there is any quantity of alcohol that might ignite at the high voltage we require. . . .

ZOYA BERYOZKINA: How can I remember all that, Comrade professor? I know he had a stomach. . . .

PROFESSOR: Ah, you don't remember anything, Comrade Beryozkina! But you can at least tell me, was he impulsive?

ZOYA BERYOZKINA: I don't know . . . perhaps . . . but not with me.

PROFESSOR: Well, well, well! I fear that while we're unfreezing him, you are freezing up! My-my-my! Well, let's proceed.

(*Presses a button. The glass door slides back silently. In the middle a shining, zinc-covered, man-sized box on an operating table. Around it are faucets with pails under them. Wires lead into the crate. Oxygen cylinders. Six calm, white-clad* DOCTORS *stand around the crate. Six washbasins in the foreground. Six towels hang, as though suspended in mid-air, on an invisible wire.*)

PROFESSOR (*to first doctor*): Switch on the current only at my signal. (*To second doctor.*) Bring the temperature up to 98.6 at intervals of fifteen seconds. (*To third doctor.*) Have the oxygen cylinder ready. (*To fourth doctor.*) Drain off the water gradually as you replace the ice with air-pressure. (*To fifth doctor.*) Raise the lid at once. (*To sixth doctor.*) Follow the stages of his revival in the mirror.

(*The* DOCTORS *nod their heads to show they have understood. They watch the temperature. Water drips. The* SIXTH DOCTOR *stares at a mirror in the right side of the crate.*)

SIXTH DOCTOR: His natural color is returning! (*Pause.*) He's free from ice! (*Pause.*) His chest is heaving! (*Pause.*) Professor, look at these unnatural spasms!

PROFESSOR (*comes up and looks closely; in a calm voice*): That's a normal movement—he's scratching himself. Evidently the parasites inseparable from these specimens are reviving.

SIXTH DOCTOR: Professor, what do you make of this? That movement of his left hand from the body. . . .

PROFESSOR (*looking closely*): He's what used to be called a "sentimental soul," a music lover. In antiquity there was Stradivarius and there was Utkin. Stradivarius made violins and Utkin played on this thing—"guitar" they called it.

(PROFESSOR *inspects thermometer and apparatus registering blood pressure.*)

FIRST DOCTOR: 98.6.

SECOND DOCTOR: Pulse 68.

SIXTH DOCTOR: Breathing regular.

PROFESSOR: To your places!

(*The* DOCTORS *walk away from the crate. The lid flies open and out comes* PRISYPKIN. *He is disheveled and surprised. He looks around, clutching his guitar.*)

PRISYPKIN: Well, I've slept it off! Forgive me, comrades, I was boiled, of course! What militia station is this?

PROFESSOR: This isn't the militia. This is the defrigeration station. We have unfrozen you.

PRISYPKIN: What's that? Unfrozen me? We'll soon see who was drunk! I know you doctors—always sniffing at alcohol! I can prove my identity; I've got my documents on me (*jumps down from crate and turns out his pockets*) . . . seventeen rubles, sixty kopecks in cash . . . paid up all my dues . . . Revolutionary Defense Fund . . . Anti-illiteracy campaign . . . Here you are, look! . . . What's this? A marriage certificate (*Whistles.*) . . . Where are you, my love? Who is kissing your finger tips? There'll be hell to pay at home! Here's the best man's receipt. Here's my union card. (*Happens to see the calendar; rubs his eyes, looks around in horror.*) May 12th, 1979! All my unpaid union dues! For fifty years! The forms I'll have to fill out! For the District Committee! For the Central Committee! My God! My wife! Let me out of here!

(*Shakes the hands of the* DOCTORS *and makes for the door. Alarmed,* ZOYA BERYOZKINA *goes after him. The* DOCTORS *crowd around the* PROFESSOR *and speak in chorus.*)

DOCTORS: What's that he was doing—squeezing **our** hands like that?

PROFESSOR: An antihygienic habit they had in the old days.

(*The six* DOCTORS *and the* PROFESSOR *thoughtfully wash their hands.*)

PRISYPKIN (*bumping into* ZOYA BERYOZKINA): For heaven's sake, who are you? Who am I? Where am I? You wouldn't be Zoya Beryozkina's mother? (*Turns his head at the screech of a siren.*) Where the hell am I? Where've they put me? What is this? Moscow, Paris, New York??? Cab! (*Blaring of automobile horns.*) Not a soul in sight! Not a single horse! Just automobiles, automobiles, automobiles! (*Presses against door, scratches his back, gropes with his hand, turns around, and sees a bedbug crawling from his collar onto the white wall.*) A bedbug! My sweet little bedbug, my darling little bedbug, my own little bedbug! (*Plays a chord on guitar and sings.*) "Leave me not, abide with me awhile . . ." (*Tries to catch bedbug with his hand, but it crawls away.*) "We part like ships in the sea . . ." He's gone! . . . . I'm all alone! "No one replies, alone I am again, alone . . ." Cab! Automobiles! . . . Seventeen Lunacharsky Street, no luggage . . . (*Clutches his head, swoons into the arms of* ZOYA BERYOZKINA, *who has run out after him.*)

SCENE 7

(*A triangular plaza. Three artificial trees. First tree has green square leaves on which stand enormous plates with tangerines. Second tree has paper plates with apples. Third tree has open perfume bottles shaped like pine cones. Sides: glass-fronted buildings. Long benches running along the sides of the triangle. Enter* REPORTER *and four other people, men and women.*)

REPORTER: Over here, comrades! In the shade! I'll tell you about these grim and astonishing events. In the first place . . . Pass me some tangerines. How right the municipality was to make the trees tangerine today. Yesterday it was pears—so dry, insipid, unnutritious!

(GIRL *takes a plate of tangerines from the tree. The people sitting on the bench peel them, eat them, and turn expectantly to the* REPORTER.)

FIRST MAN: Well, come on, comrade, let's have all the details.

REPORTER: Well, the . . . how juicy they are! Want some? Well, okay, here's the story. . . . How impatient you are! . . . Naturally, as dean of the correspondents I know everything. . . . Look, look! See that? (*A* MAN *with a box full of thermometers walks quickly through.*) He's a vet. The epidemic's spreading. As soon as it was left alone this resurrected mammal made contact with the domestic animals in the skyscraper, and now all the dogs have gone mad. It taught them to stand on their hind legs. They don't bark or frisk around any more—all they do is "beg." They pester everybody at mealtimes, whining and fawning. The doctors say that humans bitten by these animals will get all the primary symptoms of epidemic sycophancy.

ALL: O-h!

REPORTER: Look, look!

(*A* MAN *staggers past. He is loaded with hampers containing bottles of beer.*)

PASSER-BY (*singing*):
Back in the nineteenth cent-ury
A fella could live in lux-ury
Drinking beer and drinking gin
His nose was blue and hung down to his chin!

REPORTER: See? That man's sick—finished! He's one of the one hundred and seventy-five workers of the Second Medical Laboratory. To make its transitional existence easier the doctors ordered the resurrected mammal to be fed with a mixture that is toxic in large doses and repulsive in small ones—"beer" it's called. The poisonous fumes made them dizzy and some of them took a swig of it by mistake, as a refresher. Since then they've had to change the working personnel three times. Five hundred and twenty workers are in the hospital, but the terrible epidemic continues to rage, mowing everybody down on its foaming path.

ALL: A-h!

MAN (*dreamily and longingly*): I don't mind sacrificing myself in the cause of science. Let them inoculate me with a dose of this mysterious illness!

REPORTER: He's done for, too. . . . Quiet! Don't startle this sleepwalker! . . . (GIRL *comes by. She stumbles through the steps of a foxtrot and the Charleston and mutters verses from a booklet held between two fingers of one outstretched hand. She holds an imaginary rose between two fingers of the other hand. Presses it to her nose and inhales imaginary fragrance.*) Poor girl. She lives next door to this crazed mammal and at night, when the town is asleep, she hears the throb of his guitar through the wall—and then there are long heart-rending sighs and sobs. What was it they called this sort of thing? "Crooning," wasn't it? . . . It was too much for the poor girl and she began to go out of her mind. Her parents were heartbroken and called in the doctors. The professors say it's an acute attack of an ancient disease they called "love." This was a state in which a person's sexual energy, instead of being rationally distributed over the whole of his life, was compressed into a single week and concentrated in one hectic process. This made him commit the most absurd and impossible acts.

GIRL (*covers her face with her hands*): I'd better not look. I can feel these "love" microbes infecting the air!

REPORTER: She's finished, too. The epidemic is taking on oceanic proportions. (*Thirty* CHORUS GIRLS *dance onto the stage.*) Look at this thirty-headed centipede! Just think, this raising of the legs is what they (*he turns to the audience*) called art! (*A foxtrotting couple comes on.*) The epidemic has reached it . . . its—what's the word?—(*looks in dictionary*) its "apo-gee." . . . Well, this is nothing less than a hermaphrodite quadruped.

(DIRECTOR *of zoo runs in. He is carrying a small glass case. After him comes a crowd of people armed with telescopes, cameras, and fire ladders.*)

DIRECTOR (*to all*): Seen it? Seen it? Where is it? Oh, you've seen nothing! A search party reported they saw it here about a quarter of an hour ago. It was making its way up to the fourth floor. Its average speed is one and a half meters an hour, so it can't have got very far. Comrades, search the walls immediately!

(*The searchers extend their telescopes. The people sitting on the benches jump up and, shading their eyes with their hands, peer into the distance. The* DIRECTOR *gives instructions.*)

VOICES: This the way to find it? We should put a naked man on a mattress in every window. It goes for humans. . . .
Don't shout! You'll frighten it away!
I won't give it to anybody if I find it!
Don't you dare; it's public property! . . .

EXCITED VOICE: Found it! Here it is, crawling . . . !

287

(Binoculars and telescopes are all focused on one spot. The silence is interrupted only by the clicking and whirring of cameras.)

DIRECTOR: Yes . . . that's it! Put guards around it! Firemen, over here!

(People with nets surround the place. The firemen put up their ladder and people clamber up in Indian file.)

DIRECTOR *(lowering telescope. In tearful voice):* It's got away! . . . Crawled to the next wall. . . . SOS! It'll fall and kill itself! Volunteers! Heroes! This way!

(The ladder is run up a second wall. People climb up. Others watch with bated breath.)

EXCITED VOICE *(from above):* Got it! Hurrah!

DIRECTOR: Quick! Careful! Don't let it go! Don't crush the insect's legs! *(The insect is passed down the ladder and handed to the DIRECTOR. He puts it in the glass case and flourishes it over his head.)* My thanks to you, comrades, for your humble efforts on behalf of science! Our zoo has been enriched by a *chef-d'oeuvre.* . . . We have captured a most rare specimen of an extinct insect which was extremely popular at the beginning of the century. Our city may be justly proud of itself. Scientists and tourists will flock to us. . . . Here in my hands I have the only living specimen of *bedbugus normalis.* . . . Move back there, citizens, the insect has fallen asleep, it has crossed its

288

legs and wishes to rest! I invite all of you to the solemn opening of an exhibition in the Zoological Garden. The capture, so supremely important and so fraught with anxiety, has been successfully completed!

SCENE 8

(*A room with smooth, opalescent, translucent walls. Hidden, bluish lighting from the ceiling. A large window on the left. A large table in front of the window. On the right, a bed let down from the wall. On the bed, lying under the cleanest of blankets, is* PRISYPKIN. *He is filthy. Electric fans.* PRISYPKIN'S *corner is like a pigsty. The table is littered with cigarette butts and overturned bottles. A piece of pink paper has been stuck on the reading lamp.* PRISYPKIN *is groaning. A* DOCTOR *paces the room nervously.*)

PROFESSOR (*entering*): How's the patient?

DOCTOR: I don't know, but I feel terrible. If you don't order a change of staff every half-hour he'll infect everybody. Every time he breathes, my legs give way! I've put in seven fans to disperse his breath.

PRISYPKIN: A-a-a-a-a-a-a-h! (PROFESSOR *runs over to him.*) Professor! Oh, profes-s-s-or!!! (PROFESSOR *takes one sniff and staggers back, clawing the air from dizziness.*) Give me a drink. . . . (PROFESSOR *pours a little beer into a glass and hands it to him.* PRISYPKIN *raises himself on his elbows. Reproachfully.*) You resurrect me and now you make fun of me! Like giving lemonade to an elephant!

PROFESSOR: Society hopes to raise you up to a human level. . . .

PRISYPKIN: To hell with society and to hell with you. I didn't ask you to resurrect me. Freeze me back!

PROFESSOR: I don't know what you're talking about! Our lives belong to the collective and neither I nor anybody else . . .

PRISYPKIN: What kind of a life is it when you can't even pin a picture of your best girl on the wall? The tacks break on this goddamn glass. . . . Comrade professor, give me a drink. . . .

PROFESSOR (*filling glass*): All right, only don't breathe in my direction.

(ZOYA BERYOZKINA *comes in with two piles of books. The* DOCTORS *talk with her in a whisper and leave.*)

ZOYA BERYOZKINA (*sits next to* PRISYPKIN *and unpacks books*): I don't know whether this is what you want. Nobody knows anything about what you asked for. Only textbooks on horticulture have anything about roses, and daydreams are dealt with only in medical works—in the section on hypnosis. But here are two very interesting books more or less of your period—Hoover: *An Ex-President Speaks* . . . translated from the English.

PRISYPKIN (*takes the book and hurls it aside*): No . . . I want something that . . . plucks at my heartstrings. . . .

ZOYA BERYOZKINA: Well, here's a book by someone called Mussolini: *Letters from Exile.*

PRISYPKIN (*takes it and throws it aside*): No, that's not for the soul. . . . I want something that gives me that melting feeling . . . leave me alone with your crude propaganda.

ZOYA BERYOZKINA: I don't know what you mean . . . heartstrings, melting feeling. . . .

PRISYPKIN: What is all this? What did we fight for? Why did we shed our blood, if I can't dance to my heart's content—and I'm supposed to be a leader of the new society!

ZOYA BERYOZKINA: I demonstrated your bodily movement to the director of the Central Institute of Calisthenics. He says he's seen things like that in an old collection of French post cards, but now, he says, there isn't even anybody to ask about it. Except a couple of old women—they remember, but they can't demonstrate it because of their rheumatism.

PRISYPKIN: Why then did I bother to acquire such an elegant education? I could always *work* before the revolution.

ZOYA BERYOZKINA: Tomorrow I'll take you to see a dance performed by twenty thousand male and female workers on the city square. It's a gay rehearsal of a new work-system on the farms.

PRISYPKIN: Comrades! I protest! I didn't unfreeze for you to dry me up! (*Tears off the blanket, jumps out of bed, seizes a pile of books and shakes them out of the broadsheet in which they are*

292

wrapped. He is about to tear up the paper when he looks at it more closely. He runs from lamp to lamp, studying the text.) Where . . . where did you get this?

ZONA BERYOZKINA: It was being distributed to everybody in the streets . . . they must have put copies in all the library books. . . .

PRISYPKIN: Saved!! Hurrah!!

(*He rushes to the door, waving the paper like a flag.*)

ZOYA BERYOZKINA (*alone*): And to think that fifty years ago I might have died on account of this skunk. . . .

SCENE 9

(*Zoo. In the center a platform on which stands a cage draped with a cloth and decked with flags. Two trees behind the cage. Behind the trees two more cages with elephants and giraffes. On the left of the cage a rostrum and on the right a grandstand for guests of honor.* MUSICIANS *standing around the cage.* SPECTATORS *approaching it in groups.* STEWARDS *with armbands assign them to their places according to profession and height.*)

STEWARD: Over here, comrades of the foreign press! Closer to the platform! Move over there and leave room for the Brazilians! Their airship is now landing at Central Airport. (*Steps back and admires his arrangement of the guests.*) Comrade Negroes, mix in with the Britons and form nice multicolored groups with them. . . . Their Anglo-Saxon pallor will set off your complexions to even greater advantage! High school students, over there to the left. Four old people from the Union of Centenarians have been assigned to you. They will supplement the professor's lecture with eyewitness accounts. . . .

(*Two* OLD MEN *and two* OLD WOMEN *are wheeled in in wheelchairs.*)

FIRST OLD MAN: *I* remember like it was now . . .

FIRST OLD WOMAN: No, it's me who remembers like it was now!

SECOND OLD WOMAN: You remember like it was now, but I remember like it was before.

SECOND OLD MAN: But I remember like it was before, like it was now.

THIRD OLD WOMAN: I remember how it was even before that, a long, long time before!

THIRD OLD MAN: I remember how it was before *and* like it was now!

STEWARD: Quiet there, eyewitnesses, no squabbling! Clear the way, comrades, make way for the children! Over here, comrades! Hurry, hurry!

CHILDREN (*marching in a column and singing*):
We study
        all day
But we know
        how to play
We're through
        with math
And now we're off
        to see the giraffe
We're going
        to the zoo
Like the
        grown-ups do!

STEWARD: Citizens who wish to please the exhibits and also to examine them for scientific purposes are requested to obtain various exotic products and scientific equipment from the official zoo attendants. Doses prepared without expert knowledge can be fatal. We ask you to use only the products and equipment supplied by the Central Medical Institute and the Municipal Laboratories of Precision Engineering.

(ATTENDANTS *walk around the zoo and the theater*.)

FIRST ATTENDANT:
    Comrade, when looking at germs
    Don't be a dope!
    Use a magnifying glass or a microscope!

SECOND ATTENDANT:
    Take the advice of Doctor Segal
    If accidentally spat upon
    Be sure to use diluted phenol!

THIRD ATTENDANT:
    Feeding time's a memorable scene!
    Give the exhibits alcohol and nicotine!

FOURTH ATTENDANT:
    Feed them with their favorite liquor!
    They'll get gout and cirrhosis of the liver!

FIFTH ATTENDANT:
    Give them nicotine in liberal doses!
    A guarantee of arteriosclerosis!

SIXTH ATTENDANT:
    Please give your ears the best protection.
    These earphones filter every crude expression!

STEWARD (*clearing a way to the rostrum*): The chairman of the City Soviet and his closest colleagues have left their highly important duties to attend our ceremony. Here they come to the strains of our ancient national anthem. Let's greet our dear comrades!

(*All applaud. A group of* PEOPLE *with briefcases crosses the stage. They bow stiffly and sing.*)

PEOPLE:
The burdens of our office
Never tire or age us
There's a time for work
And a time for play
Greetings from the Soviet,
Workers of the Zoo!
We're the city fathers
And we're proud of you!

CHAIRMAN OF CITY SOVIET (*mounts rostrum and waves a flag; hushed silence*): Comrades, I declare the ceremony open. The times in which we live are fraught with shocks and experiences of an internal nature. External occurrences are rare. Exhausted by the events of an earlier age, mankind is glad of this relative peace. All the same, we never deny ourselves a spectacle, which, however extravagant it may be in appearance, conceals a profound scientific meaning under its multicolored plumage. The unfortunate incidents which have taken place in our city were the result of the incautious admittance in our midst of two parasites. Through my efforts, as well as through the efforts

297

of world medicine, these incidents have been eradicated. However, these incidents, stirring a distant memory of the past, underscore the horrors of a bygone age and the difficulties of the world proletariat in its mighty struggle for culture. May the hearts and souls of our young people be steeled by these sinister examples! Before calling on him to speak, it is incumbent upon me to move a vote of thanks to the director of our Zoo, who has deciphered the meaning of these strange occurrences and turned these ugly phenomena into a gay and edifying entertainment. Hip-hip . . . Hurray! Hip-hip . . . Hurray!

(*All cheer. The musicians play a fanfare as the* DIRECTOR *climbs to the rostrum. He bows on all sides.*)

DIRECTOR: Comrades! I am both delighted and embarrassed by your kind words. With all due consideration for my own part in the matter, it is incumbent upon me to express thanks to the dedicated workers of the Union of Hunters, who are the real heroes of the capture, and also to our respected professor of the Institute of Resurrection, who vanquished death by defrigeration. However, I must point out that it was a mistake on the part of our respected professor that led directly to the misfortunes of which you are aware. Owing to certain mimetic characteristics, such as its calluses and clothing, our respected professor mistakenly classified the resurrected mammal not only as a representative of *homo sapiens,* but even as a member of the highest group of the species—the working class. I do not attribute my success entirely to my

298

long experience of dealing with animals and to my understanding of their psychology. I was aided by chance. Prompted by a vague, subconscious hope I wrote and distributed an advertisement. Here is the text:

"In accordance with the principles of the Zoological Garden, I seek a live human body to be constantly bitten by a newly acquired insect, for the maintenance and development of the said insect in the normal conditions to which it is accustomed."

VOICE FROM THE CROWD: How horrible!

DIRECTOR: I know it's horrible . . . I was myself astonished by my own absurd idea . . . yet, suddenly, a creature presents itself! It looks almost human . . . well, just like you and me. . . .

CHAIRMAN OF CITY SOVIET (*ringing his bell*): Comrade director! I must call you to order!

DIRECTOR: My apologies, my apologies! Of course, I immediately established from my knowledge of comparative bestiology and by means of an interrogation that I was dealing with an anthropoid simulator and that this was the most remarkable of parasites. I shall not go into details, particularly as you will see it all for yourselves in a moment, in this absolutely extraordinary cage. There are two of them: the famous *bedbugus normalis* and . . . er . . . *bourgeoisius vulgaris*. They are different in size, but identical in essence. Both of them have their habitat in the musty mattresses of time.

Bedbugus normalis, having gorged itself on the body of a single human, falls under the bed.

Bourgeoisius vulgaris, having gorged itself on the body of all mankind, falls onto the bed. That's the only difference!

While after the Revolution the proletariat was writhing and scratching itself to rid itself of filth, these parasites built their nests and made their homes in this dirt, beat their wives, swore by Bebel,[1] and relaxed blissfully in the shade of their own jodhpurs. But of the two, *bourgeoisius vulgaris* is the more frightening. With his monstrous mimetic powers he lured his victims by posing as a twittering versifier or as a drooling bird. In those days even their clothing had a kind of protective coloration. They wore birdlike winged ties with tail coats and white starched breasts. These birds nested in theater loges, perched in flocks on oak trees at the opera to the tune of the *"Internationale,"* rubbed their legs together in the ballet, dressed up Tolstoy to look like Marx, hung upside down from the twigs of their verse, shrieked and howled to a disgusting degree, and—forgive the expression, but this is a scientific lecture—excreted on a scale far in excess of the normal small droppings of a bird.

Comrades! But see for yourselves!

(He gives a signal and the attendants unveil the cage. The glass case containing the bedbug is on a pedestal. Behind it, on a platform, is a double bed. On the bed, PRISYPKIN *with his guitar. A lamp with a yellow shade hangs above the cage. Above* PRISYPKIN's *head is a glittering halo composed of post cards arranged fanwise. Bottles lying on the floor*

and spittoons placed around the sides of the cage, which is also equipped with filters and air-conditioners. Notices saying: 1) Caution—it spits! 2) No unauthorized entry! 3) Watch your ears—it curses! Musicians play a fanfare. Bengal lights. The crowd first surges back and then approaches the cage, mute with delight.)

PRISYPKIN:
On Lunacharsky Street
There's an old house I know
With staircase broad and neat
And a curtain at the window!

DIRECTOR: Comrades, come closer, don't be frightened—it's quite tame. Come, come, don't be alarmed. On the inside of the cage there are four filters to trap all the dirty words. Only very few words come out and they're quite decent. The filters are cleaned every day by a special squad of attendants in gas masks. Look, it's now going to have what they called "a smoke."

VOICE FROM CROWD: Oh, how horrible!

DIRECTOR: Don't be frightened. Now it's going to "have a swig," as they said. Skripkin, drink!

(PRISYPKIN *reaches for a bottle of vodka.*)

VOICE FROM CROWD: Oh, don't, don't! Don't torment the poor animal!

DIRECTOR: Comrades, there's nothing to worry about. It's tame! Look, I'm now going to bring it out of the cage. (*Goes to the cage, puts on gloves, checks his revolver, opens the door, brings out* PRISYPKIN *onto the platform, and turns him around to face the guests of honor in the grandstand.*) Now then, say a few words, show how well you can imitate the human language, voice, and expression.

(PRISYPKIN *stands obediently, clears his throat, raises his guitar, and suddenly turns around and looks at the audience. His expression changes, a look of delight comes over his face. He pushes the* DIRECTOR *aside, throws down his guitar, and shouts to the audience.*)

PRISYPKIN: Citizens! Brothers! My own people! Darlings! How did you get here? So many of you! When were you unfrozen? Why am I alone in the cage? Darlings, friends, come and join me! Why am I suffering? Citizens! . . .

VOICES OF GUESTS:
The children! Remove the children!
Muzzle it . . . muzzle it!
Oh, how horrible!
Professor, put a stop to it!
Ah, but don't shoot it!

(*The* DIRECTOR, *holding an electric fan, runs onto the stage with the attendants. The attendants drag* PRISYPKIN *off. The* DIRECTOR *ventilates the platform. The musicians play a fanfare. The attendants cover the cage.*)

DIRECTOR: My apologies, comrades . . . my apologies. . . . The insect is tired. The noise and the bright lights gave it hallucinations. Please be calm. It's nothing at all. It will recover tomorrow. . . . Disperse quietly, citizens, until tomorrow. Music. Let's have a march!

CURTAIN

(1928-1929)

NOTES

Selected Poetry

I

[1] These four poems, under the general title *I*, comprised Mayakovsky's first published book. They were lithographed, in pamphlet form, at the expense of the author, in 1913, in an edition of three hundred copies. Mayakovsky designed the cover himself, and personally delivered the pamphlets to the booksellers. The pamphlets sold out at once and created considerable commotion in the Moscow literary world.

[2] *Shustov:* A Moscow cognac concern.

[3] *Avanzo:* A Moscow art dealer who exhibited pictures in his shopwindow.

The Cloud in Trousers

[1] Mayakovsky began working on this poem in 1914, and after completing it in 1915, read it aloud to Maxim Gorky. In his autobiography Mayakovsky recalled that the novelist was so moved "he wet my whole waistcoat with tears."

Publishing a poem with so many blasphemous allusions was clearly a problem in 1915. "Only Brik gave me joy," wrote Mayakovsky, "he bought all my poems at fifty kopecks a line. . . . *The Cloud* proved feathery. The censor blew right through it: six pages full of . . . Since then I hate dots, and commas too."

The censor forced Mayakovsky to change the original title of the poem, which was *The Thirteenth Apostle.* "Do you want to get hard labor for it?" asked the censor. Mayakovsky replied that the notion did not appeal to him.

According to one story of Mayakovsky's, the idea of calling the poem *The Cloud in Trousers* occurred to him when someone asked how he was able to combine lyricism with extreme coarseness of expression. Mayakovsky said: "All right, if you wish, I can be like a man possessed, but I can also be the most tender person in the world, like a cloud in trousers."

But he tells quite another version in his essay "How to Make Verse" (1926): "Around 1913, when returning from Saratov to Moscow, I tried to prove the purity of my intentions to a young woman I met on the train by telling her that I was not a man, but a cloud in trousers. As soon as I had uttered these words I knew I could use them for a poem, and that they might be repeated, wasted. Terribly worried, I began to ask the woman leading questions for a good half hour. I didn't calm down until I felt certain that my words had already gone in one ear and out the other. Two years later I needed 'a cloud in trousers' for the title of a poem."

In a foreword to the second edition of *The Cloud,* Mayakovsky wrote: "I consider *The Cloud in Trousers* a catechism for the art of today. It is in four parts, with four rallying cries: "Down with your love!"; "Down with your art!"; "Down with your social order!"; "Down with your religion!"

[2] *Maria:* In Part 1 "Maria" refers to a girl Mayakovsky had known during a visit to Odessa. The "Maria" in Part 4 is quite another person. (See note 16.)

[3] *Gioconda:* An allusion to the theft of the Mona Lisa from the Louvre in 1911.

[4] *god:* Shortly after the Revolution, by official decree, the word "God" was ordered spelled with a small *g.* Here and in subsequent passages, the English translation follows the usage as it appears in the facing Russian text.

[5] *Krupps:* The German munitions-makers.

[6] *golden-mouthed:* In the Russian Orthodox Church this expression is used to describe unusually eloquent preachers, especially St. John Chrysostom.

[7] *Petrograd, Moscow, etc.:* Mayakovsky traveled regularly across the country giving recitations of his verse.

[8] *his precursor:* Mayakovsky is comparing himself to St. John the Precursor, i.e., St. John the Baptist.

[9] *Burlyuk:* The painter David Burlyuk (1882-   ), who was a friend and futurist colleague of Mayakovsky's. Burlyuk is blind in one eye.

[10] *yellow shirt:* Mayakovsky's futurist garb.

[11] *Severyanin:* The poet Igor Severyanin (1887-1942). Although Severyanin was a futurist, "true" futurists considered him cheap and superficial because he was given to lauding the high life ("pineapples in champagne" and "lilac ice cream") in his verses.

[12] *Iron Chancellor:* In the Russian text the reference is directly to Bismarck.

[13] *Galliffet:* Gaston de Galliffet, the French general who helped suppress the insurrection of the Paris Commune in 1871.

[14] *Mamai:* Khan of the Golden Horde at the end of the fourteenth century, during the Tartar domination of Russia. After battle Mamai was fond of feasting while seated on the backs of bound Russian prisoners.

[15] *Azef:* Evno Azef (1869-1918), the notorious *agent provocateur* who played a double game, engineering the assassination of imperial ministers and betraying revolutionaries to the czarist police. He was exposed and fled abroad in 1908.

[16] *Maria:* "Maria" was, in reality, a Moscow painter and writer with whom Mayakovsky was involved during this period. After her suicide in 1919, Mayakovsky wrote a scenario which contained a scene that satirized the tragedy.

[17] *Presnya:* A rather sordid working-class street (and district) in Moscow where Mayakovsky lived.

[18] *Tiana:* A character in a poem by Severyanin.

[19] *ki-ka-pou:* An exotic dance that was currently popular in Russian night clubs. It was apparently inspired by the American Kickapoo Indian medicine shows which traveled about in Europe in the 1890's.

[1] This poem was written in the fall of 1915 with the title *Verses to Her*. Later renamed, the poem was dedicated to Lily Brik, whom Mayakovsky had recently met with her husband, the editor Osip Brik. The first public reading of *The Backbone Flute*, in 1915, before a group of thirty-six people, including Gorky, was a miserable flop. Mayakovsky required a larger audience; his thundering voice and dramatic delivery were unsuited to intimate gatherings. Some people tittered during Mayakovsky's recitation. Close to tears, the poet fumbled his lines, then fled the podium. Gorky, however, was much impressed. "After all, there's nothing much to futurism," he said. "There's only Mayakovsky. A poet. A great poet." In February 1916 Osip Brik published *The Backbone Flute* in an edition of six hundred copies.

[2] *Hoffmann:* E. T. A. Hoffmann's fantastic, ghostly tales were extremely popular in Russia.

[3] *Nevsky:* Nevsky Prospect, the main thoroughfare of St. Petersburg.

[4] *On a crag:* In these lines, Mayakovsky is evidently comparing his fate to that of Prometheus, who was chained to a mountain in Mayakovsky's native Caucasus.

[5] *Strelka:* An island resort on the Gulf of Finland, near St. Petersburg, which was a popular meeting-place for the Petersburg upper classes. *Sokolniki:* This park is a favorite promenade of Muscovites.

[6] *Lily:* Mayakovsky means Lily Brik.

[7] *Byalik:* Chaim Nachman Byalik (1873-1934), the Hebrew poet, who was a native of the Ukraine. His best-known work in Russian translation was concerned with ancient Jewish lore.

[8] *Albert:* King of Belgium during World War I, when Belgium was almost entirely occupied by the Germans.

To His Beloved Self, the Author Dedicates These Lines

1 This poem was written early in 1916, and was ultimately published in 1918 in the almanac of the Spring Salon of Poets, in Moscow.

An Extraordinary Adventure which Befell Vladimir Mayakovsky in a Summer Cottage

1 This poem was written in June 1920 at the cottage in Pushkino (twenty-seven versts from Moscow) which Mayakovsky had rented for the summer. He apparently liked the company there so much that he continued to rent the cottage for several more summers.

2 *Rosta:* The Russian Telegraphic Agency, where Mayakovsky was employed drawing posters and cartoons. During the period of his most intensive work for Rosta, from October 1920 to February 1922, Mayakovsky made 2,000 drawings and 280 posters on all kinds of domestic and international events. He captioned his drawings with jingles and slogans that became famous at the time.

Order No. 2 to the Army of the Arts

1 Mayakovsky's second "order" was written in 1921. The first (1918) was an equally hortatory utterance: "Comrades! To the barricades!" he urged, "Streets are our brushes/ squares our palettes."

2 *futurists, imaginists, acmeists:* Members of avant-garde literary movements of the 1910's.

3 *Proletcult:* The Proletarian Cultural Educational Organization, founded in 1918, was supposed to urge proletarians to produce class-conscious literature. The movement failed largely because the proletarians produced poor imitations of their bourgeois predecessors.

4 *Rosta:* See *An Extraordinary Adventure,* note 2.

I Love

[1] This poem, which Mayakovsky dedicated to Lily Brik, was written in 1922, during their love affair. It was published the same year in an edition of two thousand copies. A second edition, published in Latvia shortly after, was seized as pornography by the Latvian police.

[2] *Müller:* The author of a popular calisthenics manual.

[3] *Rion:* A river in Georgia near Mayakovsky's birthplace.

[4] *"three leaves":* A card game.

[5] *Kutaisi:* The region in Georgia where Mayakovsky was born.

[6] *Butyrki:* A notorious Moscow prison in which Mayakovsky was held for eleven months in 1909-10, for participating in underground Bolshevik activities.

[7] *"Funeral Parlor":* Such an establishment was visible from the windows of Butyrki.

[8] *Cell 103:* The number of his cell at Butyrki.

[9] *Ilovaiskys:* D. I. Ilovaisky, the author of history textbooks that were standard in Russian schools.

[10] *Dobrolyubov:* Nicholas Dobrolyubov (1836-1861), a radical literary critic. The name means "a lover of good."

[11] *Sadovayas:* The Sadovaya is a boulevard, composed of several sections, which rings Moscow.

[12] *Passion Square:* Moscow's Strastnoi Square, named after the Monastery of Christ's Passion nearby.

[13] *Maupassant's archetype:* The reference is to Maupassant's story, "An Idyll," in which a nursing mother shares a railway compartment with a hungry peasant boy. The breasts of the woman, who is traveling without her baby, swell up agonizingly, until the boy gratefully relieves her of her milk.

[14] *covetous knight:* Pushkin's play *The Covetous Knight* (1830), a classical study of avarice.

Brooklyn Bridge

[1] This poem was written in 1925 during Mayakovsky's three-month stay in the United States.

[2] *Hudson:* Mayakovsky confused the Hudson with the East River.

Back Home

[1] Mayakovsky began writing this poem on board the French ship *Rochambeau,* which sailed from New York to Le Havre from October 28 to November 25, 1925. The poem's original title was *Marquita.*

[2] *Gosplan:* State Planning Commission, the organization responsible for drawing up the national economic plan.

[3] The final lines of the poem echo the Central Committee report made by Stalin at the 14th Congress of the All-Union Communist Party (Bolsheviks) in December 1925. These final lines were substituted at the last minute for the original ending, which read: "I want to be understood by my country,/but if I fail to be understood—/what then? /I shall pass through my native land/to one side,/like a shower/of slanting rain."

Conversation with a Tax Collector about Poetry

[1] This poem was written in May 1926, and published the following month in Tiflis. Mayakovsky often recited it when he lectured on "how to make verse."

[2] *forty pounds of table salt:* The Russian saying is: "In order to know a man, one must eat forty pounds (one pood) of salt with him." In other words, one must spend as much time with him—eating and drinking—as it takes to consume forty pounds of salt.

[3] *Bagdadi:* Mayakovsky's birthplace.

[4] *But, after all:* In the original this line has an untran-

slatable allusion to the saying, approximately: "Every head finds its own hat."

[5] *N.K.P.S.*: People's Commissariat of Communications.

[6] *hiccup*: An allusion to a Russian saying: "When someone hiccups a dead man is remembered."

Letter from Paris to Comrade Kostrov
on the Nature of Love

[1] This poem was written in November 1928 during a brief stay in Paris, where Mayakovsky had fallen in love with Tatiana Yakovleva, an eighteen-year-old Russian émigrée. The poem is dedicated to her. Comrade Taras Kostrov, the editor of *Young Guard*, had commissioned Mayakovsky to write political poems from Paris for his magazine. Published in *Young Guard*, in January 1929, the poem was angrily received by the authorities.

[2] *cupolas*: The reference is to the cupolas on Russian Orthodox churches.

[3] *Copernicus*: Mayakovsky means that only great men, like Copernicus, are rivals worthy of him. *Maria Ivanna*: The most common of Russian surnames and patronymics (Ivanna is the colloquial form of Ivanovna, or daughter of Ivan).

At the Top of My Voice

[1] This poem, written in January 1930, was Mayakovsky's last important work. He intended it to be Part 1 of a two-part introduction to a longer poem. Part 2 was to have been lyrical, in contrast to the nonlyrical Part 1.

[2] Mayakovsky had drawn health posters which urged people to drink boiled water against epidemics.

[3] *Myself a garden*: Two lines from a type of popular Russian ditty or *chastushka*.

[4] *curly Macks . . . clever Jacks*: Literally, "curly Mitreikas and clever Kudreikas." Mayakovsky was poking fun here

at two young poets, K. Mitreikin and R. Kudreiko, whom he had criticized recently at a writers' conference.

5 *Tara-tina:* A line from a "trans-sense" poem, *Gypsy Waltz on the Guitar,* by the constructivist poet Ilya Selvinsky.

6 *Agitprop:* The Agitation and Propaganda Section of the Central Committee of the Communist Party, in charge of political indoctrination.

7 *Esenin super-hero:* This is a crack at the poet Sergei Esenin's (1895-1925) messianic bent.

8 *posters:* Mayakovsky is referring to the hundreds of propaganda posters he drew during his lifetime.

9 *CCC:* Central Control Commission of the Soviet Communist Party.

Past One O'clock

1 After Mayakovsky's suicide on April 14, 1930, this poem was found, untitled, among several pages of scribbled lines in his notebook. It is presumed to be either a continuation of *At the Top of My Voice* or part of the projected lyrical introduction to that poem. Mayakovsky used the middle quatrain as an epilogue to his suicide note, with one significant alteration: he changed the "you" to "life" in the line, "Now you and I are quits." The epilogue therefore reads: "And, as they say, the incident is closed./Love's boat has smashed against the daily grind./Now life and I are quits. Why bother then/to balance mutual sorrows, pains, and hurts."

2 *The Milky Way streams silver:* In the original, the Milky Way is compared to the Oka River, an affluent of the Volga.

3 *I have no cause:* In another version found in Mayakovsky's notebook, this line is followed by: "The sea pulls back again/the sea pulls back to sleep." The poem then continues as it appears in the text printed in this volume.

4 *the incident is closed:* Even in his suicide note Mayakovsky could not resist a pun. He altered the cliché phrase, *intsident ischerpan,* meaning "the incident is closed," to

intsident isperchen, suggesting that "the incident is too highly peppered," or too spicy, and hence spoiled.

The Bedbug

[1] *The Bedbug (Klop)* opened at the Meyerhold Theater in Moscow on February 13, 1929, and remained in the repertoire until May 16, 1930. Its director was Vsevolod Meyerhold, with Mayakovsky as assistant director. Meyerhold thought highly of the author. "Mayakovsky knew what theater is . . ." he wrote, "he was not only a brilliant playwright but also a brilliant director. I have been staging plays for many years but I never allowed myself the luxury of letting a dramatist work with me directing a play. But not only did I permit Mayakovsky to work with me, but I found I could not work without him."

The incidental music for the original production of *The Bedbug* was composed by Dmitri Shostakovich. The composer recalls that Mayakovsky asked him to write a score that would be suitable for a "local firemen's band." Although this was not exactly in Shostakovich's line, he did his best. On hearing the music for the first time, Mayakovsky merely remarked: "Well, in general, it will do." The score has since been lost.

Mayakovsky began writing *The Bedbug* in the fall of 1928 during his travels to Germany and France, and completed it in Moscow at the end of December 1928. He had been in a great hurry to finish the play and rush back to Paris to meet Tatiana Yakovleva, with whom he had fallen in love. On December 28 he wrote in a letter to Tatiana: "We—your Waterman and I—have written a play. We read it to Meyerhold. We wrote it twenty hours a day without food and drink. My head got swollen from this kind of work—even my cap won't fit any more. . . . I work like a bull—my mug with its red eyes lowered over the desk. . . . I still have mountains and tundras of work and I'm finishing it off and I'll rush to see you."

Mayakovsky had another, incidental reason for rushing *The Bedbug;* he was longing to make enough money to buy a Renault automobile in Paris and bring it back to Moscow. Although Mayakovsky succeeded in buying the Renault, the play was a disappointment in every other respect. He tried unsuccessfully to sell the play to a German publisher and to the German producer Erwin Piscator. It failed in Moscow, and in Leningrad as well, where it was performed at the Great Drama Theater in 1929.

After 1929 *The Bedbug* was produced only a few times and for very brief runs. Then, in May 1955, it was staged with tremendous success by Sergei Yutkevich and Valentin Pluchek at Moscow's Satire Theater. Since 1955 it has been in the repertoire of Russian theaters in most major cities of the Soviet Union, and in 1960 was running simultaneously at the Satire Theater and the Mayakovsky Theater in Moscow.

The Bedbug was produced at the Provincetown Theatre in New York in 1931.

Scene 1

1 *private peddlers:* Some forms of private enterprise were allowed between 1921 and 1928 under Lenin's New Economic Policy (NEP).

2 *Nobile:* Umberto Nobile, Italian Arctic explorer whose dirigible crashed after a flight over the North Pole in 1928. The survivors were picked up by a Russian icebreaker.

3 *Mr. Ryabushinsky:* The Ryabushinskys were a family of Moscow millionaires.

4 *Plekhanov:* Georgi Plekhanov (1857-1918), outstanding theorist of Marxism.

5 *"Kiss, kiss!":* Literally, "bitter, bitter" (*gorko*). An ancient Russian custom at weddings. The guests demand that the

bride and groom give each other a sweet kiss to sweeten
the bitter vodka the guests are drinking.

Scene 2

[1] *Pierre Skripkin:* The hero has changed his name from
the ridiculous-sounding Prisypkin to what he imagines to be
the more elegant Skripkin, derived from *skripka* (violin).
Ivan has become Pierre, in imitation of the practice, among
the Russian upper classes, of assuming French first names.
[2] *Apukhtin:* Alexis Apukhtin (1841-1893), a worldly, sen-
timental poet despised by Mayakovsky.
[3] *Nadson:* Semyon Nadson (1862-1887), a melancholy, senti-
mental poet equally despised by Mayakovsky, and the fre-
quent butt of his jokes.
[4] *Liebknecht:* Karl Liebknecht (1871-1919), German Socialist
leader.
[5] *Nepmen:* Private businessmen during the NEP (New
Economic Policy).
[6] *Suvorov:* Alexander Suvorov (1729-1800), celebrated Rus-
sian field marshal who was never defeated in battle.

Scene 3

[1] See Scene 1, note 5.
[2] *Perekop:* A Bolshevik force crossed the Straits of Perekop
and drove the White armies out of the Crimea in Novem-
ber 1920.
[3] *Botchkin:* In the original, Oleg has changed his name from
the comical-sounding Botchkin, derived from *botchka* (bar-
rel) to the poetic *Bayan* (a Russian minstrel of ancient
times). Mayakovsky was making fun of a minor poet he had
known before the revolution, Vladimir Sidorov, who had
actually adopted the pen-name Bayan.
[4] *Kamarinsky:* A Russian folk dance.

5 *"Makarov's Lament for Vera Kholodnaya"*: The lady was a famous Russian silent movie actress.

6 *Whites:* Men of the White Army, which opposed the Red Army during the Civil War.

Scene 4

1 *Nadson and Zharoff:* Semyon Nadson, see Scene 2, note 3. Alexander Zharoff (1904-   ), a militant Communist poet, and another frequent target of Mayakovsky's.

Scene 9

1 *Bebel:* August Bebel (1840-1913), a founder of the German Social-Democratic Party.